HALFWAY HOME

A Comedy in Two Acts

by

Diane Bank

SAMUEL FRENCH, INC.

45 WEST 25TH STREET   NEW YORK 10010
7623 SUNSET BOULEVARD HOLLYWOOD 90046
LONDON   TORONTO

No one shall commit or authorize any act or omission by which the copyright of, or the right to copyright, this play may be impaired.

No one shall make any changes in this play for the purpose of production.

Publication of this play does not imply availability for performance. Both amateurs and professionals considering a production are *strongly* advised in their own interests to apply to Samuel French, Inc., for written permission before starting rehearsals, advertising, or booking a theatre.

No part of this book may be reproduced, stored in a retrieval system, or transmitted in any form, by any means, now known or yet to be invented, including mechanical, electronic, photocopying, recording, videotaping, or otherwise, without the prior written permission of the publisher.

IMPORTANT BILLING AND CREDIT REQUIREMENTS

All producers of HALFWAY HOME *must* give credit to the Author of the Play in all programs distributed in connection with performances of the Play and in all instances in which the title of the Play appears for purposes of advertising, publicizing or otherwise exploiting the Play and/or a production. The name of the Author *must* also appear on a separate line, on which no other name appears, immediately following the title, and *must* appear in size of type not less than fifty percent the size of the title type.

3

Halfway Home was first produced at The New Group Theatre in New York City in October 1993; under the direction of Scott Elliott; with the following cast:

SUSAN MILHALOVIC	Donna Mitchell
MARGE MILHALOVIC	Judy Frank
ANNE COOPER	Jill Bowman
CAROL MILHALOVIC	Marie Masters
NICK	John Wojda
BABBY TORKELSON	Amy Stiller
BRENDA MILHALOVIC	Olivia Birkelund
GWEN MONROE	Roma Maffia

Production design; set and costumes: Zaniz
Technical Director and lighting design: Francis X. Lockwood
Production Stage Manager: Michelle Malloy Mcintyre
Assistant Stage Manager: Rob Bogue

CHARACTERS

SUSAN MILHALOVIC — Thirty-five. Tour guide. Feisty, though charming. Tries very hard to keep it together.

MARGE MILHALOVIC — Late fifties. Maternal. Overbearing. Always tries to put on a happy face.

CAROL MILHALOVIC — Thirty-eight. A CPA. Cool. Controlling. Superior.

ANNE PORTER — Twenty-nine. Housewife. Eight months pregnant. The mother of three already. Is prone to crying jags, laughing fits and food binges. It's her hormones.

BRENDA MILHALOVIC — Thirty-one. Nurse. Reserved. Timid.

GWEN — Twenty-eight. A nurse. Brenda's roommate and companion. Tall, dark and handsome. Honest and upfront. Rides a motorcycle.

BABBY TORKELSON — Marge's next door neighbor. Checker in a supermarket. Self-effacing. Unsure of herself. Easily impressed.

NICK — Forties. Cab driver. Been around, or so he says. Unflappable. Game for anything.

TIME & PLACE

Prologue:
A tour bus in New York City. August. The hottest day of the year.

ACT I
A living room in Ankeny, Iowa. Thirty-six hours later.
A taxi on Interstate 80.

ACT II
Scene 1: The living room. A moment later.
Scene 2: The living room. An hour later.

AUTHOR'S NOTE

The movement of the play should be extremely fluid. The prologue on the New York tour bus can be performed downstage in front of the curtain facilitating the set change to the Iowa living room.

In the New York production the taxi cab scenes were played behind the picture window. And during the taxi set change, photographic slides of cities, road signs, etc. were shown on the drawn window shade to depict the cross country trip. The taxi scenes can actually be played anywhere on the stage that will facilitate a smooth and rapid set change in and out of them. In moving from one scene to another, dialogue or music can be used in the blackout. Any apropos country music will do. The same applies for Act II when Nick serenades the room with a ballad.

Above all, the play is a comedy, even in the moments which touch on the dramatic, it remains a comedy. The pace is quick and the style heightened.

HALFWAY HOME

PROLOGUE

LIGHTS UP on a Manhattan tour bus stuck in traffic on Broadway. It is the hottest day of summer and the bus air conditioning is not working. SUSAN, the tour guide stands center. ED, the bus driver, is indicated, but unseen. SHE speaks to the audience as though they are the bus riders.

SUSAN. (*Clapping her hands.*) People! People! Could I have your attention, please? C'mon, people, listen up! Ed, our bus driver, has informed me that we've hit a little snag in traffic here. So, if you'll all just relax in what soon will be air conditioned comfort, I'm sure we'll be moving shortly. An interesting footnote: Today officially marks the longest, hottest heat wave in the Metropolitan area on record. Isn't that something! Another exciting tidbit to tell the folks back home about the greatest city in the world. New York, New York—city of dreams where even the unspeakable is possible. So! While we're stopped, why don't I tell you a little bit about what we'll be seeing on our tour today. As I said at the start, my name is Susie, celebrating seven years with "Smile Tours." Seven years to the *day,* in fact, and I'll be your guide. Your driver, of course is, Ed. Say hello again, Ed. And *this* is the 9 a.m. Super Deluxe Tour Package #5, exploring lower Manhattan and the Statue of Liberty. Soon, we'll be on our way and our next stop, aside from this one, will be China Town where we'll visit a real, live Buddhist Temple/souvenir shop and dine at an authentic Chinese take-out restaurant. Do you have take-out where you're all from? (*No response.*) Take-out? (*No response.*) You know like, take-out? (*Still, no response.*) Oh well, doesn't matter. (*Clapping.*) Everybody! If you'll look out the bus windows you'll see one of things New York is famous for—traffic! This is rush hour and in New York rush hour means— well, it means we're stuck is what it means. Uh ... Ed, could you double check the air, please? It's getting a teensy bit warm in here. Oh! Important rush hour tip... (*SHE indicates someone in the audience.*) You. Yes, you. The person I'm pointing at—*you*. You must sit *down*. Sit down. Thank you. And relax. Be patient, and think happy thoughts like the natives do. So, here we are on Broadway. Broadway! Forty-second Street. The lights. The glamour. Dreams realized. Hopes dashed. Once we get moving, I want you to look down the side streets. All the world-famous Broadway Theatres are on either side. So, why do they call it "On Broadway" if all the theatres are on the side streets? Anybody? It's really easy. No one? Alright. *Because* the theatres used to be on Broadway. Simple, isn't it? Can you all hear me okay? Because I know you can't hear me if you're talking. I talk. You listen. That's the way we do things in New York. (*Points to someone in the audience.*) Sir? Sir? For your safety and the safety of your fellow passengers, please remain seated at all times. Please sit down. Sit down. Sit down. (*SHE gestures for him to sit.*) Sit! Thank you. Ed, could you bump up the air conditioning a little? Ed? The air when you get a chance? So! Then after China Town we'll go to the renowned

Statue of Liberty. (*Dramatically.*) The Statue of Liberty. Huddled masses yearning to breathe. Big. Green. It's really quite something to see ... eventually. Let's see, WhatelseWhatelseWhatelse? Oh, look! There's something interesting. Out the window on your left. Left. (*SHE points out the window.*) Left! There's a bum. That's right, folks, a genuine New York City street person. Right there on your *left*. Isn't he a character? He may have been a doctor once, or a stock broker, or a tour guide. New York, New York—you're down one day, up the next. So! Is anybody else suffocating? No, seriously, until we start moving which will be very, very, *very* shortly I'm sure, why don't we get acquainted? Won't that be fun? Let's get a little give and take going, shall we? So, where are you all from? Your home? Where is it? If nobody answers I'm going to have to pick somebody. Okay, you asked for it. (*SHE points to someone in the audience.*) How about you—lady in black? Yes, you. *Where are you from? Your home?* South Yemen? Oh. South Yemen. Fascinating. People! We have someone here from South Yemen. Welcome to the Melting Pot. Apt description for today, huh? Anybody else? (*SHE points to someone.*) You, sir? Yes, the gentleman-who-is-talking-while-I-am-talking— where are you from? South Yemen? You're from South Yemen, too? Isn't that a coincidence? Only in New York, right folks? South Yemen ... wow ... (*SHE looks over the audience.*) You wouldn't *all* be from South Yemen, by any chance, would you? (*SHE looks about nodding and smiling.*) Yes? My, my ... I guess the tour director forgot to mention that. So, your English is, at best—(*SHE makes a so-so hand gesture.*) poco, poco? English? Nonexistent? Yes? Great! That's great! South Yemen. That's near Yemen, isn't it? Gosh, it's a small planet! Ed, aren't you from South Yemen? Oh, I'm sorry, South Bronx, of course. I knew that. So ... I'm from Iowa. Iowa? The midwest? USA? Corn, tires, insurance, J.C. Penney's?

I still have family there. And vague memories. And stories I can't quite recall. I don't even remember what Iowa looks like anymore. Isn't that funny? Yep, I came here umpteen years ago to make it. To be wildly successful. To do *something*, at least. And let me tell you, it was thrilling. The ups, the downs, the disappointments, the confusion—you have no idea. But that's a whole other bus ride ... Iowa ... wow ... People say hello to you on the street there. Complete strangers—"Hi! How are you?" They smile as they pass. And everything is fine. Even if it isn't. Not like here. Not at all like here. God, I wish we could open a window or something. But, you know what? You want to know a secret? A big secret? Want to know what they don't tell you in the brochure? The windows? They don't open. They're welded shut. So, if there was a fire, or a front end collision, or snipers, or we couldn't breathe or something—tough luck. Adios. Good to know. It's good to know. And you want to know another secret? A deep, dark secret? I mean, since we're getting so chummy and all—I lie about my age. I do. I confess. I lie. I'm thirty-one. Thirty-three, if we want to be totally accurate. Actually, thirty-five, if we want to get real picky. Thirty-five years old. And look where I am today, to the *day*, to the *minute*. You know, you could at least look in my general direction when I talk. You could *pretend* to be interested, at least. I might as well be a monkey with a little hat and a cup dancing for your enjoyment, huh folks? Now, *that* you would like, wouldn't you? Hey Ed, crank up the organ, the natives are getting restless! These people need entertainment! Okay, you asked for it—I'm single. I'm a registered Democrat. I've had two abortions. I live in a tiny, hole-in-the-wall on the West Side. My cat died. My boyfriend went back to his ex-wife. I've been mugged twice. I'm an insomniac. I go to the movies every Friday night. I make just enough money to squeak by. And I have an extensive and intimate knowledge of the largest and most wonderful cesspool in the world. Ah, New York, New York—just when you think you know it all. Just when you think you've seen it all, felt it all. New York, New York—city of curve balls and low blows. City of people who don't speak English, right folks? Who pee wherever the hell they feel like it. Who sneak up behind you. Look right through you. (*SHE points to someone in the audience*.) City of people who don't sit down. Sit down! *Sit down!* Look in the eyes of someone who's had it up to here. Because just this morning I thought, "It's going to be one of those days, Susan." I remember I was packing my purse at the time. "Yep, another one of those days ....," I said to myself. Better be on guard. Better be prepared. Don't forget: lipstick, compact, billfold, keys. Better be one step ahead this time.

Anticipate impending disaster. Don't forget: deodorant, aspirin, moist towelettes, mace. And for that extra protection, for real peace of mind—(*SHE pulls a gun out of her purse*.)—your basic .38 caliber nine shot revolver. Capiche? Comprehendo? So, sit down!!! We all should've stayed at home with our goats and mud huts and people who love us. Because, we're not going anywhere. No egg rolls and ferry boat rides for us. No cheery, "Hi! How are you's?" We're stuck. We're bumper to bumper. Broken minds and bodies and spirits all around us. Snipers on the rooftops. And the windows don't open and there's only so much air in any given space. You're going to suffer, people. You better get used to it. Life—where you're down, but never quite dead. Life—trampled, bloody, bowed—you come crawling back for more. And you wonder, "WHAT THE HELL AM I DOING HERE?" (*SHE indicates someone in the audience. SHE points the gun.*) And as for you? I said, sit down. Sit down. *Sit ... down!*

(*SUSAN points the gun. LIGHTS FADE to BLACK. There is the sound of a GUNSHOT. A moment, then still in DARKNESS we hear the Muzak version of a cheery song interspersed with the sounds of LIGHTNING and THUNDER. LIGHTNING AND THUNDER FADE out as the MUSIC continues.*)

ACT I

SCENE: The living room of Marge Milhalovic's house in Ankeny, Iowa. It is cozy and simple. Stage right is a small dining room table with four chairs. Up right is an archway which leads to the kitchen where the telephone is located. Upstage center is a sofa flanked by two end tables with lamps. In front of the the sofa is a long coffee table. On the upstage wall is a large picture window with a shade. Stage left is an archway through which the front door is visible. Upstage and to the left of the front door is the exit to the basement. Also stage left in partial view are stairs leading to the second floor where the bedrooms and bathroom are located. There are also several chairs against the walls. On all the tables are bowls of snacks: Potato chips, M&Ms, popcorn, Cheese Doodles.

AT RISE: Hung from the ceiling is a banner which reads: "WELCOME HOME SUSAN!" MARGE is sitting at the dining room table on top of which is a large watermelon cut in half. SHE is using a melon-baller to scoop out the melon which SHE does throughout the act. Also on the table is a RADIO. An easy-listening station is playing the instrumental version of a cheery song. CAROL and ANNE, Marge's daughters, are also in the room. CAROL is sitting on the sofa reading the newspaper and ANNE, who is obviously pregnant, is standing by the window looking out. SHE is eating a

15

candy bar. [NOTE: ANNE eats snacks constantly throughout the play, especially when upset.] Pause. MUSIC plays.

MARGE. (*Closing her eyes and chanting mantra-like.*) It's going to be fine. It's going to be fine. Everything's going to be fine. Fine. Everything fine. (*SHE opens her eyes and turns off the RADIO. SHE looks around the room. SHE speaks calmly and in control.*) Girls, I want you to listen to me. Very important. We're all going to act normal. Can we please do that? Can we act normal? Can we at least try? Anne, come away from that window and straighten the banner. It's crooked.

ANNE. (*Looking out the window.*) Babby's out in her yard. She's just standing there. Just standing there looking up at the sky.

MARGE. Normal—that's the theme for today. Just another normal day. We're all going to act natural.

ANNE. (*Out the window.*) What is she doing out there anyway?

MARGE. Natural—that's the key word. Everything's fine. And happy. We're all together and happy. And today's a wonderful day.

ANNE. (*Out the window.*) She's going to get drenched if she stays out there in this. Drenched or struck by lightning.

MARGE. When Susan walks through that door we're going to be calm. And sitting. We'll all be sitting. Sitting and eating fruit. Because there's nothing like a fruit boat for festive occasions. All those wonderful colors and textures. And it's relaxing. Balling fruit is very relaxing. Busy hands, busy mind. Now, all I need is Brenda with those cantaloupes and I'll be all set. Yes sir, a wonderful day.

ANNE. Maybe Babby doesn't know about the tornado.

MARGE. Anne, come away from the window.

ANNE. In a trailer park of all places. They were finding mobile homes as far as Des Moines.

MARGE. Where on earth is Brenda with the fruit? I need more fruit.

ANNE. Five people dead and others missing, the radio said.

MARGE. She called two hours ago and said she'd be here with the fruit.

ANNE. Maybe I'd better go tell Babby.

MARGE. You leave Babby alone. We've got work to do. Now, straighten that banner like I asked. Carol, help your sister.

CAROL. (*From behind the newspaper.*) The banner looks fine, Mom.

MARGE. It's crooked. Am I the only one who can see it's crooked?

CAROL. It's fine.

ANNE. Mom thinks it's crooked.

MARGE. (*Under her breath.*) It is crooked.

CAROL. (*Putting the paper down.*) Excuse me for venturing an opinion, but do you think having this little party is really a good idea? I mean ... considering? I mean, considering Susan?

MARGE. What do you mean?

CAROL. I mean, considering the fact she's crazy?

ANNE. Crazy?

MARGE. She's not crazy. Don't you dare say that. Susan is not crazy. You know I hate that word.

ANNE. She's not crazy, Carol.

MARGE. She's your sister, for heaven's sake.

CAROL. She's always been crazy. I mean, she drops off the face of the earth for years, and now this? Nobody hears a word from her in God knows how long, then you get some urgent, cryptic telegram?

MARGE. Cryptic? It wasn't cryptic.

CAROL. (*Recites telegram.*) "Dire straights. Must lie low. Driving in on Saturday."

MARGE. It means she misses us. It means she's finally come to her senses. And she didn't drop off the face of the earth. She's been busy.

CAROL. For ten years?

MARGE. Well, it's not like we didn't get Christmas cards. Don't forget the Christmas cards.

CAROL. Yeah, one a year for ten years. Reach out and touch, huh?

MARGE. She's busy with her job—

CAROL. What job? We don't even know what she does.

ANNE. Well, whatever it is, it's very important. And there's nothing wrong with her, Carol.

MARGE. That's right. And I don't want her to think we think otherwise. Everything's fine and she's perfectly alright. Period. Enough. Now, am I going to have to do everything around here myself? Am I? Because I will. I'll do everything myself if I have to.

CAROL. Fine. I'll straighten the banner. (*Crosses to banner.*)

MARGE. No, I'll do it. I don't mind.

CARCL. Annie, give me a hand.

MARGE. If it's too much to ask, I'll do it.

CAROL. Annie?

ANNE. (*Looking out the window.*) It's really starting to pour. Babby's still out there.

CAROL. Annie? Now. Now, Annie.

(ANNE helps CAROL straighten the banner.)

MARGE. And I wouldn't worry about the weather. The Farmer's Almanac said bright and sunny for today. Bright and sunny.

ANNE. Can you imagine? Mobile homes as far as Des Moines?

MARGE. I bet Susan's on the interstate right now driving into town. I bet she'll be here any minute. What I want to know is—where is Brenda with the fruit? I can't make a fruit boat without fruit.

ANNE. Why not?

MARGE. Without fruit?

CAROL. Brenda will be here. She was probably just held up in a bloody wreck.

ANNE. (*Laughs at the "joke."*) Oh, God …

MARGE. Carol, I know you're trying to lighten things up, but please, not now. (*Looks at the banner.*) Now, that's what I call straight. That's nice. Isn't that lovely? "Welcome home Susan." You did a nice job, Anne. The flowers on the border were a wonderful touch. You were always so artistic. Too bad nothing ever came of it. Now, what am I forgetting?—film for the camera, clean sheets on the bed, extra towels, a fresh tube of toothpaste in the bathroom. What is it? Girls? What am I forgetting?

CAROL. I don't know, Mom. (*SHE goes back to reading the newspaper.*)

MARGE. What am I forgetting, Anne?

ANNE. I need a cookie.

MARGE. This isn't about you, dear. This is about Susan. I'm forgetting something about Susan.

CAROL. And I don't think cookies for breakfast is wise or rational, do you? Especially in your delicate condition.

ANNE. I'm craving cookies. It's a *craving*.

CAROL. Is that what you call it?

MARGE. Oh, I wish I could remember what it was I forgot. I should've made a list. There's just so much to think about. Oh, isn't this excitement exciting? I'm getting goosebumps. All of us together. In one place. All of us talking and laughing. And listening. Listening is very important. And acting interested. Carol, please put down the newspaper.

ANNE. This woman in my Lamaze class? She ate wallpaper paste.

MARGE. What?

ANNE. Wallpaper paste. She ate a whole bucket. She craved it. She ate it.

CAROL. Wallpaper paste?

ANNE. I mean, you of all people, should understand "cravings," Carol. "CRAVINGS." I mean there is a reason why we're serving lemonade instead of champagne, isn't there?

MARGE. Stop it, Anne. Right now. You know better than that. I'm surprised at you.

ANNE. All I'm saying is, a person can do crazy things and not be actually crazy. Not be totally "irrational." Like cookies. Like wallpaper paste. Like Susan. Like everybody sometimes.

CAROL. (*To Marge.*) What is she talking about?

(The PHONE in the kitchen rings.)

MARGE. Oh my goodness, that's probably Susan. *(SHE gets up and takes breath.)* Oh, my … *(SHE slowly sits back down.)*

CAROL. Let me get it.

MARGE. It's Susan. I know it is.

CAROL. Mom, sit. Just sit and take it easy. I'll get it. *(SHE exits to kitchen.)*

MARGE. *(Calling after her.)* Tell her we're all waiting. Tell her we're thrilled. Annie, it's Susan.

ANNE. It's Susan!

CAROL. *(Calling from kitchen.)* It's Brenda!

MARGE. *(Calling.)* Who?

CAROL. *(Calling.)* Your daughter Brenda?

MARGE. *(Calling.)* Oh, Brenda! Where on earth is she?

CAROL. *(Calling.)* She says she's running a little late. *(Beat.)* And she says they're out of fruit at the A&P.

MARGE. *(Calling.)* What?

CAROL. *(Calling.)* THEY'RE OUT OF FRUIT!

MARGE. *(Calling.)* Well, tell her to try the Farmer's Market. And if that doesn't work, try Mr. Dees 7-Eleven. *(To herself.)* I swear I have to think of everything myself …

CAROL. *(Enters with the phone receiver on a long cord.)* She wants to know if you realize there's a tornado watch?

MARGE. Oh, let me talk to her. *(Takes the receiver. As SHE exits to kitchen:)* Brenda, what is your problem!

(MARGE exits to kitchen. CAROL goes into the living room.)

CAROL. Brenda must've had a rough night.

ANNE. She's just going through a phase at the moment.

CAROL. A what?

ANNE. A difficult phase.

CAROL. Is that what Mom said?

ANNE. As a matter of fact, she did. And I agree.

CAROL. And great minds, well ... I guess it must be true then.

MARGE. *(Entering from kitchen.)* Well, that's straightened out. Sometimes I wonder about that girl ...

CAROL. Oh, really?

ANNE. There's nothing wrong with her, Carol. And There's nothing wrong with Susan, either. You think there's something wrong with anybody who acts different than you. You're just jealous. Everybody knows it.

MARGE. Anne!

CAROL. Oh, really? Jealous?

ANNE. That's right. Jealous. Jealous.

MARGE. Girls, stop it. Just stop it. Nobody's crazy. Nobody's different. Nobody's anything. We're nothing—all of us—nothing. Now, let go. Everybody, let go. We have more important things to think about ... if I could just remember what they were ... I'll tell you what though, everything's falling into place. Just like I planned. That's the secret to a great party. Planning. And execution. Always a step ahead. We used to have such great parties. Remember? Birthday parties. Graduation parties. Wakes. People, still to this day, talk about your father's funeral.

About how cheery it was. How well I held up. And several even asked for the recipe for my spinach dip. That's called positive thinking. Turning something horrible into something wonderful. And if there's one thing I can give my children as my legacy, it's that—the power of positive thinking. Because that's our heritage. That's where we come from. My mother's mother's mother came here in a covered wagon. And we're not talking about "Little House on the Prairie," either. We're talking about drought and locusts and influenza. They farmed the land with their bare, bleeding hands. (*Getting a bit overwhelmed.*) My mother's mother made—

(*Beat.*)

    MARGE/CAROL/ANNE. —soap.
    MARGE. She actually slaughtered a pig and made—
    MARGE/CAROL/ANNE. —soap.
    MARGE. Pig fat and lye soap. They didn't have time to worry about their skin in those days. And the only thing that kept them from curling up in a ball and being blown away with the dust was family. And hope. Hope. The ability to reach down into the gunk of life and pull out a handful of sunshine. (*Eerily cheerful.*) Hello, sunshine! Bright and sunny! Hello, disaster! Hello, destruction! Hello! *That,* is my legacy to my children.
    CAROL. Jealous … that's a good one …
    ANNE. Jealous, jealous.
    MARGE. Carol dear, would you mind getting me a Bromo?
    CAROL. Are you alright?

MARGE. My stomach's acting up a bit. Please dear, a Bromo? It's in the upstairs bathroom. And there's a drinking glass on my night table.

CAROL. (*Starts to go, stops.*) You're not going to talk about me while I'm out of the room, are you?

MARGE. Of course, not!

CAROL. Alright. (*SHE exits up stairs.*)

MARGE. (*Waits until Carol is out of ear shot. Whispering.*) Poor Carol ...

ANNE. (*Whispering.*) She's going to ruin this, you know.

MARGE. No, she's not.

ANNE. She likes to ruin things.

CAROL. (*Calling from upstairs.*) I hear whispering.

MARGE. (*Calling.*) No, you don't, dear! (*To Anne, whispering.*) She's not going to ruin anything.

ANNE. I worked on the banner all night.

MARGE. (*Smoothing Anne's hair.*) And it's lovely. You're my right hand, Annie.

ANNE. I am?

MARGE. My right hand. I depend on you more than anybody. Just remember, you have children, Carol doesn't.

CAROL. (*Calling from upstairs.*) I'm still hearing whispers!

MARGE. (*Calls.*) Nobody's whispering, honey! (*To Anne, whispering.*) And Poor Carol, well, it's just her nature to be contentious and sarcastic and contrary. We have to be understanding. Understanding is the key.

ANNE. So, you want me to humor her? Is that what you're saying?

MARGE. Oh heavens, no. Just ignore her. That's what I do.

CAROL. (*Calling from upstairs.*) I'M COMING DOWN NOW! (*Enters with Bromo.*)

MARGE. (*Loudly.*) It's a lovely banner, Anne. (*Takes the Bromo from Carol.*) Oh, thank you, dear. See how sweet we can be if we try? (*Toasts.*) Cheers, everyone. To family. (*SHE drinks it down.*)

CAROL. Family ... right ... Well, at least now I know what a person has to do IN THIS FAMILY to get a party. Nobody ever threw me a party in the last twenty years. I'm too sane. I'm too stable. I have a career. I stayed here. I didn't run off. I plodded along. I inched my way forward. On my belly. In the trenches. I didn't mess up. I achieved. A certified public accountant. That means something in this world. CPA. I can do numbers in my head. In my *head*. I don't even need a calculator. And guess what else? I just got a promotion. Did you know that? No, you didn't. And why? Because you don't ask. That's why. "Oh, another promotion? That's nice."—yawn. Good, old Carol. No muss, no fuss. Dependable, responsible, always on time. (*As if calling a dog.*) Here, girl. Here, girl. Fetch, Carol, fetch. But, I'm sorry. This is about Susan, isn't it? Susan. Isn't it, Mom? This isn't about me.

MARGE. What isn't?

CAROL. Nothing. (*Beat.*) By the way, I said I got another promotion.

MARGE. Yes, and it's wonderful. Isn't it wonderful, Anne?

ANNE. What?

CAROL. Oh, never mind!

MARGE. You know, Anne, maybe you'd better give Tom a call and check on the children. I think that would be good idea, don't you? After all, you know Tom ...

ANNE. Yes, Tom ... I don't know how a man who's such a good district manager of a farm machinery plant can be such an inept caregiver. It's beyond me. You're right, I'd better call. Yes, I'd really better ... (*SHE stands a moment.*)

MARGE. Well, go on then.

CAROL. Yes, go on, Annie.

ANNE. You're not going to talk about me, are you? (*SHE slowly exits.*)

MARGE. Oh, for heaven's sake. Would you go call? (*Calling after her as SHE exits.*) Check and see if the party hats are in the cupboard. (*To Carol.*) Poor Annie ...

CAROL. Poor Annie ... such a mess.

MARGE. (*Confidentially.*) Well, God love her, she tries ...

CAROL. She just gets so—

MARGE. —on a person's nerves. Believe me, I know. It's her condition.

CAROL. Yes, and isn't it comforting to note that she's the sole guardian of the family gene pool?

MARGE. Oh, you'll have kids yourself one of these days. All my girls'll have children. Even Brenda.

CAROL. Brenda? Hello, Mom?

MARGE. Brenda's just taking a little detour on the path of life.

CAROL. Well, she's got a new friend on the path, did you know that?

MARGE. A little detour, that's all.

CAROL. An acquaintance of mine saw them on the street, hand in hand—tall, dark, and handsome from what I've heard ...

MARGE. And that detour's going to wind around right back onto the main highway, just you wait and see. Period! (*Beat.*) Oh, isn't this nice? It's so quiet and peaceful.

ANNE. (*Loudly, from the kitchen, the sound of an argument.*) I *SAID*, I'LL BE HOME WHEN I'M HOME! I'M BUSY!

(*MARGE keeps her attention on the kitchen.*)

CAROL. (*Sits next to Marge on the sofa.*) Mom, about Susan ... She didn't leave here under the best of circumstances. Remember? The way she left? On the day of Dad's funeral? Just leaving like that? (*SHE lays her head on Marge's shoulder.*)

ANNE. (*Loudly, from kitchen.*) SHUT UP!

CAROL. (*Takes Marge's hand.*) She hasn't been here for a very long time. I just hope you're not going to be disappointed, that's all.

MARGE. Disappointment isn't in my vocabulary, dear.

CAROL. I bet she hasn't changed a bit.

MARGE. (*Pulling her hand away.*) This isn't a contest.

ANNE. (*From kitchen.*) THAT'S RIGHT! SHUT UP!

MARGE. And how dare you think that I don't appreciate you! I do. You're my right hand, Carol. My right hand. And you know what else? We'll throw you a party, too. One of these days. I promise. When you get a promotion or something. Won't that be nice? Now, about, Annie—

ANNE. (*Loudly, from kitchen.*) FUCK YOU! FUCK YOU! FUCK YOU!

MARGE. Just try to be a little more understanding, alright?

CAROL. (*Taking her hand.*) Mom, you're not listening to me.

MARGE. (*Pulling her hand away.*) Of course, I'm listening. I always listen. What on earth is wrong with everybody today?

(*BLACKOUT on living room.*
LIGHTS UP on taxi. It is on the interstate. NICK is driving. SUSAN is sitting in the back leaning forward onto the front seat. SHE is holding a gun close to Nick's face. SHE is wired, but exhausted and straining to stay awake.)

SUSAN. What did you say your name was again?

NICK. Nick.

SUSAN. Nick—that's right. Nick. Don't be scared, Nick. Just keep driving and you won't get hurt.

NICK. Would you mind … ?

SUSAN. What?

NICK. The gun? I'm operating a vehicle here.

SUSAN Oh, sorry. (*SHE moves the gun. SHE leans in to him.*) I'm a very dangerous person, Nick. I'm a desperate, dangerous, sleepy person. So, I wouldn't try anything funny if I were you. No quick moves. No sudden hand gestures. You do what I say and we'll get along fine. (*The gun is near his face.*)

NICK. (*Indicating the gun.*) Would you mind?

SUSAN. (*SHE moves the gun. SHE leans in to Nick.*) Yes, a very dangerous, lethal person, Nick. So, don't get any bright ideas. Don't even think about it. Just be quiet and drive. (*SHE waves the gun near his face.*)

NICK. WOULD YOU GET THAT GODDAMNED GUN OUT OF MY FACE!

SUSAN. Don't yell at me!

NICK. JESUS CHRIST!

SUSAN. Stop yelling at me!

NICK. I think you better give me a damn good reason right now why I shouldn't pull over.

SUSAN. I have a gun!

NICK. Yeah, well don't we all? (*HE pulls out a gun and lays it on the dashboard.*) But you don't see me waving it around like a maniac. So, you want me to keep driving? Convince me, or we stop right here.

SUSAN. No, wait. Wait. (*Beat. SHE takes a breath.*) Did you ever have one of those days, Nick? One of those days when everything stopped making sense? One of those incredibly rotten days which capped off an incredibly rotten succession of years. Which you weren't aware of until this one incredibly rotten day? And then suddenly—bang. A spark. A whoosh. All hell breaks loose. Did that ever happen to you?

NICK. Once.

SUSAN. So, you think if you can just get grounded again. Get back on track. But, how? Where? Someplace familiar. The eye of the storm, maybe. So, please don't pull over. Please keep driving. Please. (*Beat.*) Please?

NICK. Well finally, if it isn't the magic word ...

(*LIGHTS OUT on taxi. LIGHTS UP on living room a moment later.*)

ANNE. (*From the kitchen.*) FUCK YOU! (*There is the sound of the PHONE RECEIVER being slammed down.*

ANNE enters eating from a tub of Cool Whip.) They're all alive. Everybody's alive and well. Petey and Jane and Tom and little Chrissie. They all say hi.

MARGE. (*To Anne.*) You didn't say you loved him.

ANNE. What?

MARGE. On the phone just now. You didn't tell Tom you loved him.

ANNE. I didn't? How did you know that?

MARGE. A mother can hear a pin drop in a wind tunnel, dear. You should always say you love him, Anne. No matter what. Any moment could be the last, you know. Like with your father? When he went out to get that final pack of pipe tobacco? The last thing I said was, "I love you." The very last thing. "I love you, Bill. Don't forget to take your medication now," I said. And then he had that massive coronary on the street, face down in the gutter like that. So sudden. So ... messy. Why, sometimes I still half-expect him to come bursting through that front door, disheveled and late like always.

CAROL. Yes, it's too bad he isn't here to see all this. He just adored Susan ...

MARGE. He adored all of us, dear.

ANNE. And he was so handsome, too ...

MARGE. Anne, where are those party hats?.

ANNE. Party hats? What party hats?

MARGE. Honestly Anne, you have the shortest attention span I've ever seen.

CAROL. Aren't they a little much? I mean, really?

MARGE. I'll find them. You all just sit. I'll get them. (*Starts to go to the kitchen. SHE stops.*) Remember girls, a pin drop in a wind tunnel ... (*SHE exits.*)

*(CAROL watches her go. ANNE stands behind her eating
from the tub of Cool Whip. A moment.)*

CAROL. *(Without turning around.)* Why don't you sit
down, Anne? Party hats … good God … Next we'll be
jumping through hoops …

ANNE. *(Teasing, under her breath.)* Jealous. Jealous …

CAROL. I heard that.

ANNE. *(Under her breath.)* Carol's jealous. Carol's
jealous.

CAROL. What is wrong with you?

ANNE. Nothing is wrong with me. Why do you always
say that?

CAROL. You are so touchy sometimes.

ANNE. I'm not touchy!

CAROL. You're so strange.

ANNE. I'm pregnant.

CAROL. Well, I'm concerned. Somebody has to be.

ANNE. Concerned about what?

CAROL. Well, like Mom for starters.

ANNE. Mom?

CAROL. Don't tell me you haven't noticed.

ANNE. Noticed what?

CAROL. Look at her.

ANNE. She's happy.

CAROL. You call that happy? I call that *too* happy.
Too excited.

ANNE. What do you mean?

CAROL. *(Takes a breath.)* Susan.

ANNE. Yeah?

CAROL. Susan. Mom and Susan.

ANNE. What about them?

CAROL. You must remember what it was like.

ANNE. What what was like?

CAROL. Mom and Susan. MOM AND SUSAN. The way they WERE. WAY BACK. Do I have to spell it out for you? Think! C'mon!

ANNE. It's a void.

CAROL. A what?

ANNE. When I think back it's a void.

CAROL. What are you talking about?

ANNE. I'm saying, I don't remember much. Hardly anything. Actually, nothing. That's what I'm saying.

CAROL. You don't remember anything?

ANNE. No.

CAROL. Oh, sure you do.

ANNE. I don't.

CAROL. Are you telling me, you don't remember anything about your childhood? About growing up in this house? The fights?

ANNE. Fights?

CAROL. Mom and Susan fighting all the time?

ANNE. No.

CAROL. Or Dad? Dad in the middle? Dad always siding with Susan? His precious little Susan. *The loud, vicious fights*?

ANNE. No.

CAROL. So, you're telling me, you have no recollections whatsoever?

ANNE. None.

CAROL. You have no memories?

ANNE. No.

CAROL. This is frightening ...

ANNE. I don't remember you. Or Brenda. Or Susan. Or Mom and Dad. When I was little. Until I was about age ten. I start remembering at about age ten.

CAROL. Age ten?

ANNE. And even after that, it's hazy until ... oh ... until around high school.

CAROL. High school? So, you don't remember what it was like around here? Growing up?

ANNE. I heard it was nice.

CAROL. You heard it was nice?

ANNE. Mom always said it was. She said it was real nice.

CAROL. Well, what about the funeral? Dad's funeral? Ring a bell?

ANNE. Now, *that* I remember.

CAROL. Everyone came back here after the service. Poor Mom ...

ANNE. Mom held up very well.

CAROL. She was in shock. She was numb. And then Susan making a scene like she did.

ANNE. A scene?

CAROL. She and Mom yelling in the kitchen. And then her storming out of the house.

ANNE. Storming?

CAROL. Then, hardly a word from her in ten years. Mom hasn't been the same since. And now this ...

ANNE. What are you talking about?

CAROL. (*Recites telegram.*) "Dire straights. Must lie low. Driving in Saturday morning." The shit's gonna hit the fan once again, just you wait. And I'm going to be sure to duck, but Mom ... it's going to hit Mom square between the eyes.

ANNE. You're just trying to upset me.

CAROL. Oh, for Christ's sake! This is not about *you*!

ANNE. But, you're not going to get to me. Not today. You're just afraid Susan's going to stay. That's what you're really *concerned* about about. Jealous. Jealous.

(MARGE enters with party hats.)

MARGE. (*Holding up hats.*) Look what I found in the refrigerator, Anne. *In the refrigerator,* for heaven's sake ... Maybe we should make some confetti? Would that be too much? Or maybe colored streamers? What do you think?

(There is a POUNDING at the front door.)

MARGE. Oh, my goodness. This must be her.

ANNE. Susan?

MARGE. It's her. It's her. (*Getting up.*) Now girls, remember what I said.

CAROL. Normal and natural, was it?

MARGE. And we all love each other.

(There is more POUNDING.)

MARGE. First impressions, girls. First impressions.

CAROL. Mom?

MARGE. What, dear?

CAROL. The door? Maybe we should answer the door?

MARGE. The door! Of course! I'll get it. Let me get it. This is my house. I'll get it.

*(MARGE goes to the door with ANNE following behind.
SHE opens it. BLACKOUT.
LIGHTS UP on the taxi. NICK is driving. SUSAN is in
the backseat lying down. The audience does not see her.
NICK is singing a few bars of a country song. HE
stops singing.)*

NICK. You know what we need right now? We need
Hank Williams. No wonder the post office put him on a
stamp. Greatest singer that ever was. He's got me through
more than a few bad times, I'm not ashamed to say. Like
Mexico, for one ...

*(SUSAN sits up in the backseat. SHE is still holding the
gun. SHE leans forward, her head next to Nick's. SHE
has just awakened. SHE looks around.)*

NICK. Well, nice of you to join us. I've got a thermos
of coffee and half a jelly donut, if you want. You missed a
glorious sunrise a while back. I'm working on a second
wind, myself. Sleep well? No cricks or cramps, I hope.
SUSAN. I was dreaming of covered wagons and bare,
bleeding hands. Where are we?
NICK. Just crossed the state line. Now, isn't this is
beautiful? Beautiful! The open road. Gently rolling hills.
Mile after mile of cornfields like one big déjà vu. I must've
driven through here a hundred times on 1-80. Never stopped
though, except for fuel. Food and fuel. Always in a hurry
to get to some place. And from that place to the next place.
Something always nipping at my heels. It's in the blood. I
have nomadic blood. Gypsy blood. Nomadic, Polish,
Gypsy blood. My people are flung to the far corners. Don't

even know where anymore. And everything I own, you
may wonder?—One suitcase. Travel light. Travel fast. And
never look back, except over my shoulder, maybe. So,
nobody has to put a gun to *my* head and say, "Drive." No
sir. "One foot out the door at all times"—as my dear
mother used to say. Words to fly by. (*Beat.*) Iowa. Never
realized it was so green. Hundred times through here—
never realized it. I bet when the sun shines it's dazzling.
(*Beat.*) Now, what was I talking about? Oh yes, Mexico.
Want to hear a sad story? One to break your heart? Don't
worry, though. It's got a happy ending ... if there is such a
thing.

(*HE sings a few bars of a country song as LIGHTS FADE
    to BLACK.*
*LIGHTS UP on the living room as before. The front door
    is open and BABBY, Marge's neighbor, stands in the
    open door. HER eye is bruised and her lip is swollen.
    SHE is soaking wet.*)

MARGE. Babby?
BABBY. Hi.
MARGE. Babby?
BABBY. May I come in?
MARGE. Oh, I'm sorry, Babby. Of course you can
come in. Come in. (*To Anne and Carol.*) Relax everyone,
it's just Babby.
BABBY. (*Entering.*) Hi, everybody.
ANNE. Hi, Babby.
MARGE. Goodness, look at you.

BABBY. I was standing in the yard looking up at the clouds. I've never seen clouds as black as this. I'm locked out.

MARGE. Locked out?

BABBY. Of my house. Pretty stupid, huh? I'm an idiot.

ANNE. No, you're not. I do it all the time.

BABBY. No, I'm a total, complete idiot. A stupid, stupid idiot. I ran out of the house. The door slammed behind me. I didn't have my key. I can wait outside if you want. If I'm interrupting. I deserve to wait outside. I'll go. I'm sorry.

ANNE. You can't wait outside.

BABBY. Or in your garage. I can wait out the rain in your garage. It'd sure teach me a lesson. Anyway, I can see I'm intruding.

ANNE. You're not intruding, Babby.

BABBY. You're sure?

MARGE. We could call a locksmith for you.

BABBY. (*To Carol.*) I fell down.

CAROL. Excuse me?

BABBY. On my face. You may have noticed. I fell down. (*Beat.*) Looks pretty bad, doesn't it?

ANNE. No, not at all.

BABBY. I'm so stupid sometimes. To fall on my face like that. On the floor like that. Face-down on the kitchen tiles. And then to run out of the house like that. What a day. Boy, oh boy … What a lousy day! (*SHE laughs at her "joke." SHE crosses to the table.*) Oh, is this a fruitboat? Marge, are you making a fruitboat? Everybody loves your fruitboats! They're so festive! So, is this a party? Are you having a party? Is that what this is?

ANNE. It's Susan. Susan's coming home.

BABBY. Susan? Oh, my God! Susan? And you're giving her a party? A welcome home party? That's so nice.

MARGE. Yes, isn't it?

BABBY. Gosh, she hasn't been here in—what? How long?

MARGE. Oh, I don't know … awhile …

CAROL. Ten years.

BABBY. Ten years? Ten years?! She hasn't been home in ten years?

MARGE. It's not like we haven't heard from her.

ANNE. She sent Mom Christmas cards.

MARGE. Every Christmas.

BABBY. This family is so nice. This is the nicest family. I always wanted a family like this. A nice family in a nice, normal home. Why would anyone stay away from here for ten years? I can't imagine it.

MARGE. Why don't you call a locksmith, dear?

BABBY. A locksmith?

MARGE. To get into your house?

BABBY. To get into my house? Oh! To get into my house! To get into my house, yes, of course. No. No. That's okay. No.

CAROL. Is everything alright, Babby?

MARGE. Carol …

BABBY. I fell down.

CAROL. Yes, we know.

BABBY. I'm so clumsy. I look terrible.

CAROL. So everything's alright, then? Your Mom? (*Beat.*) Dwight?

MARGE. Carol, maybe we shouldn't pry.

CAROL. Oh, I'm sorry. Am I prying?

BABBY. Oh no, everything's fine. Fine. More than fine. Good. Things are good. And they can only get better. Dwight's still looking for work, of course, but it's looking good. And Mom, well ... Mom talks to the coat rack in the convalescent home, but she seems happy, so that's good. And uh ... uh ... I'm sorry, what did you ask me?

CAROL. Everything's fine?

BABBY. Well, I fell down, of course ...

CAROL. Yes, that's what you said.

BABBY. But other than that ... (*SHE shrugs.*) Now don't let me keep you from anything. I know you're probably very busy. I mean, of all the gosh, darn days for me to do this, to get locked out like that—I'm just so sorry. I'm so sorry. I'm so STUPID! I'm just so STUPID, STUPID, STUPID! So, incredibly STUPID!

MARGE. Babby, it's alright. Really.

BABBY. No, it's not alright! It's not!

MARGE. Why don't you just sit down and take it easy? It's so stressful forgetting one's keys.

BABBY. It's STUPID!

MARGE. Let's get you something to drink. Some tea, maybe?

BABBY. Just a Valium would be fine.

MARGE. A what?

BABBY. Valium. Ten milligrams. (*SHE reaches in her pocket and pulls out a pill vial.*) Oh, boy ... (*SHE takes a pill.*) I don't suppose anybody has an anti-depressant on them, do they?

(*There is a POUNDING on the door.*)

ANNE. Susan!

BABBY. It's Susan?

MARGE. She's here! She's here. Now remember everybody—

CAROL. Mom, the door? Mom?

MARGE. I'll get it. Everyone sit down. Sit!

CAROL. The door?

MARGE. I said, I'll get it. Now *sit down*, Carol. And be quiet. For once in your life, just be quiet. And happy. Everybody, happy. Smile!

(MARGE goes to the door and opens it. BLACKOUT.)

(LIGHTS UP on taxi downstage left. NICK is driving and SUSAN is in the backseat leaning forward looking at the road ahead.)

NICK So, there I was stranded in Tijuana working in some broken-down carnival biting the heads off chickens. The geek. The carnival geek. Talk about a dead end job. Talk about down on my luck. They don't even have geeks anymore—that's how low that job is. And with the animal rights groups and everything these days—forget about it anyway. Yep, there I was—a drunken, stinking geek. Spending every peso I could on humiliation. Hell-bent on destruction. Didn't think it was possible to fall any further. I was wrong, though. Dead wrong.

SUSAN. I was a tour guide.

NICK. And I was a geek.

(THEY laugh.)

NICK. See? If you can laugh at your own rock bottom, you know you're on the road to recovery.

SUSAN. So, what happened?

NICK. Well, the long and short of it was, I was spared. A señorita came from out of the crowd and took me by the hand and pulled me towards redemption. Saved my life.

SUSAN. Was she beautiful?

NICK. Good God, no! But anyway, the thing of it is, the hardest part is picking up the pieces after the plunge. Some people go from here to there and it's no big deal. Other people go from there to here and it's a miracle. I'm a miracle. And when I saw you the other day, when I saw you running down Broadway, well ... let's just say, I know a fellow traveler when I see one. (*A moment, then HE gently takes the gun from her hand.*) Now why don't you just sit back and relax, enjoy the ride while you can— advice from one bird to another. (*Indicates the the sky ahead.*) Well, would you look at that? Looks like we got some interesting weather up ahead.

(*SUSAN looks at Nick. HE glances at her. Then, THEY both watch the road ahead. LIGHTS FADE to BLACK.*
LIGHTS UP on the living room as before. MARGE has opened the front door. BRENDA pushes in. SHE is carrying a large grocery bag. Her rain poncho is dripping wet. SHE is enraged, but smiling, and trying to maintain control.)

MARGE. Brenda!

BABBY. It's Brenda.

CAROL. As you were everyone, it's just Brenda.

BRENDA. Don't anybody say anything. Not a word. I don't want to hear it. It's been a really INCREDIBLE morning and I'm not in the mood, okay? So YES, I'm late. I KNOW, I'm late. I've been driving in weather conditions in which I could not see my hand in front of my face let alone find the Farmer's Market which was CLOSED, by the way. CLOSED. Or MR. DEE'S 7-Eleven which had a large TREE sticking out the front window. Yes, the market was CLOSED which gave me renewed faith in the intelligence of mankind since apparently SOME people ARE smart enough to stay out of the rain. SOME people do not feel duty-bound to risk their lives for fruits and vegetables. SOME people know that when there is a TORNADO WATCH in effect that shelter is indeed a priority as opposed to, say, a party. My car stalled TWICE, and let me repeat that, TWICE. My engine was FLOODED. Which is not surprising since the rain was falling HORIZONTALLY. But, on a positive note, this is probably all great for the CROPS, but hell for my shoes which are currently filled with water and much too expensive for the likes of my paltry nurse's salary. And as an afterthought, it's important for you all to know just how extremely put-upon I'm feeling right now—not that I have to justify my feelings to anybody, family included—so, I STRONGLY suggest any opinions or criticism of my performance today be kept to yourselves.

MARGE. My goodness …

BRENDA. I'm sorry I got so angry.

MARGE. Well, we were terribly worried about you. Weren't we, girls?

CAROL. Petrified.

ANNE. I was at the window all morning.

BRENDA. Well, that helps thank you, but still—
(*Looks around.*) Where's Susan?

MARGE. She hasn't arrived yet. She should be here
any minute. That fruit came just in time.

BRENDA. Fruit?

MARGE. You brought fruit.

BRENDA. Oh, yes ... fruit. I ended up at some cult-
operated roadside stand, God knows where. A bunch of
dazed disciples, "Moonies" probably, standing in the rain
selling kiwi.

MARGE. What?

BRENDA. Kiwi.

MARGE. What's that?

BRENDA. It's Australian. It's green.

MARGE. No cantaloupes?

BRENDA. Kiwi is very popular.

MARGE. No honeydews?

BRENDA. Sorry.

MARGE. Bananas, grapes, berries, anything?

BRENDA. Kiwi.

MARGE. You know I don't trust foreign fruit.

BRENDA. Well, that's all they had left. Two dozen
kiwi. That's all I have.

MARGE. Two dozen ... kiwi? That's all you have?
That's *all*?

ANNE. (*Glancing at Carol. Softly.*) Uh oh ...

MARGE. I asked you to do one simple thing, Brenda.
One little thing.

BRENDA. Sorry, it couldn't be helped.

MARGE. It's not like I asked you to go to California
to get the fruit.

BRENDA. It couldn't be helped.

MARGE. Or Florida, *the sunshine state*, to get the fruit.

BRENDA. *It couldn't be helped.*

MARGE. Because, it's not like I ever ask you to do anything. I realize you're busy. I've heard about your active social life.

BRENDA. (*Warning her.*) I really don't think you want to get into that. Let's keep to the topic at hand. Let's stick to fruit.

MARGE. Or lack of it.

BRENDA. So, this is going to be a major issue?

MARGE. One tiny, teeny, little, simple thing. And I waited all morning. I should've done it myself. I should've.

BRENDA. It's not life and death, Mother.

MARGE. Obviously, not to you. Obviously, it means nothing to you. Obviously.

BRENDA. Are you going to blow this all out of proportion? I mean, isn't this about *Susan*? Isn't that why we're here? Because of *Susan*?

MARGE. Of course, it is.

BRENDA. Then let's not forget that, alright? This is not the end of the world.

CAROL. That's what *you* think ...

BRENDA. Don't start with me, Carol.

CAROL. Excuse me?

MARGE. Girls, please.

BRENDA. I said, don't start.

(*ANNE stifles a giggle.*)

BRENDA. You too, Anne. (*To Marge, slowly and deliberately and very reasonably.*) So, this is not going to be a big problem, is it Mother? Is it? Because if you'd like to take the time to make it a BIG problem, then I'd be happy to oblige.

MARGE. No, I guess it's not.

BRENDA. No?

MARGE. No.

BRENDA. Good. (*Looks at her watch.*) Come on now. Let's take the kiwi in the kitchen. It's going to be just fine, Mom. You'll see. Oh, by the way, there's just one, other, little thing I need to talk to you about—

(*THEY exit into the kitchen.*)

BABBY. (*Beat.*) God, this is so funny.

CAROL. Funny?

BABBY. All of us here. And Susan. Susan coming home. It's like all these memories are flooding in. Memories from way back. And Brenda just now reminded me of Susan. All that rage pouring out. I always wanted to be like that. Like Susan. To be wild and nuts like that. Free. Unencumbered. Susan got away. New York. God. She's probably all sophisticated by now. We probably all look like dopes or something. Yeah, Susan was the one. She was always the one. She was special. Don't you think she was special?

CAROL. Special?

ANNE. I think we're all special.

BABBY. But, she was special in a special way.

ANNE. We're all special in our own ways. All of us.

BABBY. It's just that Susan was different, I guess. A different kind of special. She was the one.

ANNE. The one what?

CAROL. Are you sure you don't want to call a locksmith, Babby?

ANNE. Susan never had children. I was the only one to have children.

CAROL. Oh, here we go ...

ANNE. (*To Carol.*) Well, you don't have children.

CAROL. Did it ever occur to anybody that maybe some people don't want children?

ANNE. Brenda doesn't have children either, and never will. It's me. I'm the only one.

CAROL. Some people have options. They choose not to have children. They give it an ounce of thought, at least.

ANNE. What's that supposed to mean?

BABBY. I'm barren. Dwight had mumps.

CAROL. In fact, some people don't even like children.

ANNE. What are you saying? Everybody likes children.

CAROL. Not everybody.

ANNE. How can anybody not like children? That's unnatural. You're just saying that to upset me, Carol. You always try to upset me. Always.

CAROL. Not always.

ANNE. In my condition, I'm not supposed to be upset. I'm supposed to be calm and catered to. I'm supposed to be radiant and glowing and beautiful. But, see what you've done? I'm upset. And bloated. Bloated and swollen and puffy and misshapen. I can't even make a fist. Did Mom tell you? I'm going to have to have my ring cut off. My wedding ring. I wear shoes two sizes bigger than normal now. I get blinding headaches. Double vision. Mood swings. I can't finish a complete thought. I have water on the brain. Tom sleeps on the sofa bed in the living room because he says I slosh every time I roll over. He says I *slosh*. It disturbs him. It disturbs his precious sleep. But, I can't sleep. I can't sleep because I'm afraid I'll drown in a pool of bile from the heartburn I've had since day one. Day *one*. Heartburn and morning sickness from day one. And my gums bleed. And I'm hungry all the time. And if you want to know the whole truth, I'm the one in my Lamaze class who ate the wallpaper paste. That's right. Me. I ate a whole bucket! (*ANNE goes to the window and leans looking out. SHE sniffles.*)

BABBY. Why don't you sit down, Annie?

ANNE. I can't sit down. If I sit down, I might not be able to get up. Then Carol would suggest they SHOOT me, right, Carol? (*SHE goes back to looking out the window.*)

CAROL. Of all the days to be trapped inside ... listening to this ...

BABBY. (*Confidentially to Carol.*) It's the barometric pressure.

CAROL. What?

BABBY. Everybody's on the edge of their seats. It's that kind of day. The excitement. Susan. The party. And when you add to that, barometric pressure, well ...

CAROL. Yeah ...

BABBY. People do the silliest things in weather like this. Take me, for instance. Getting locked out of my house like that. Pretty stupid. (*Including Anne, loudly.*) Pretty darn stupid, right, Annie? (*No response from ANNE. To Carol.*) And then to fall like that ...

CAROL. Fall?

BABBY. On my face like that.

CAROL. Oh.

BABBY. Right on the floor like that. The kitchen floor. Dwight about laughed himself sick.

CAROL. (*Suddenly interested.*) Dwight?

BABBY. He thought it was very funny. And it probably was. I probably looked really hilarious splayed out on the kitchen floor. Face-down like that. And he'd been drinking, too. So, it probably seemed funnier than it actually was.

CAROL. Kind of early to be drinking, wasn't it? Even for Dwight.

BABBY. Well, you know Dwight ...

CAROL. Yes, I guess, I do. Or rather, did.

BABBY. I meant "know" in the general sense. Not in the personal, biblical, drinking sense.

CAROL. I know what you meant, Babby.

BABBY. He's still fond of you, though. He talks about you all the time.

CAROL. That's nice.

BABBY. So, anyway ... uh ...

CAROL. He laughed at you?

BABBY. Yeah, he laughed for awhile, then he went to the bathroom to be sick for awhile. Eventually, he passed out hugging the toilet. That's such an ugly sight, isn't it, Carol? Somebody passed out hugging the toilet? So anyway, I was watching him there, passed out like that, and I thought ...

CAROL. (*Beat.*) What?

BABBY. I thought, "Gee, wouldn't it be swell to just ... " You know ...

CAROL. (*Beat.*) What?

BABBY. Oh, you know, to just ... push his head in the toilet and hold it there? You know, hold it there until he stopped breathing? Or hit him with something. Like an

iron? A couple of good whacks on the head with an iron.
Like the sound of a stick hitting a coconut. Kind of a
hollow, thud sound. Or maybe stab him with something.
Like a stake. Or a pitch fork. Or one of those long, scary
butcher knives. I was just standing there thinking how
swell it'd be. Don't you ever imagine killing somebody?

CAROL. No.

BABBY. Everybody does it.

CAROL. No, I don't think so.

BABBY. Oh, sure they do. All the time.

CAROL. I don't think so, Babby.

BABBY. Oh, sure. Admit it. Like your boss, maybe?
Off with his head?

CAROL. No!

BABBY. (*To Anne.*) Annie, do you ever imagine
killing Tom?

ANNE. (*Turning slowly.*) Killing Tom?

CAROL. Oh, this is ridiculous.

BABBY. Like when he's sleeping or something?

ANNE. Oh, like hitting him with a shovel? Something
like that?

BABBY. Yeah!

ANNE. Or stabbing him with a screwdriver? A dull,
painful screw driver ...

BABBY. Right through the heart!

ANNE. Right through the heart! Quick and easy!

BABBY. I'll show you quick and easy. *This* is quick
and easy! (*Makes a gun with her hand and shoots.*) BOOM!

(*ANNE and BABBY laugh.*)

CAROL. So, Dwight's ... alright?

BABBY. Dwight?

CAROL. You didn't do anything *really* silly, did you? He is alright, isn't he?

BABBY. Oh, I wouldn't worry about him. After all, you know Dwight. (*SHE laughs and takes another Valium.*) Now, I know this is family day, so if I'm in the way, just tell me. Feel free to tell me.

ANNE. You're not in the way, Babby. And even if you were, you couldn't go out in weather like this. (*Looks out the window.*) Gosh, just look at it out there. Maybe it *is* the end of the world.

(BABBY joins ANNE at the window. BRENDA bursts out of the kitchen followed by MARGE.)

MARGE. I won't hear of this. You're going to stay. Your sister will be here any minute.

BRENDA. I told you I'll be back in a little while. I have to run a quick errand.

MARGE. You're not going anywhere.

BRENDA. I have to. I don't have a choice.

MARGE. Brenda, I mean it.

BRENDA. I'm really sorry. I have to go.

MARGE. I mean it, Brenda. You had better stay right here.

BRENDA. (*Facing her squarely.*) Or what, Mom? Or what?

MARGE. (*Beat, backing down.*) Alright. Okay. Go. Go on. Leave. Run your errand, if it's so important. Put your family on the back burner. We're used to it, aren't we, girls? It's just too bad, that's all. You were so dependable once. You used to be my right hand, Brenda. My right hand.

ANNE. Right hand?

CAROL. Excuse me?

MARGE. I just don't understand the rush, that's all. Why can't whatever it is just wait? Especially when Susan will be here any minute. What's your hurry anyway?

BRENDA. (*Heading for the door.*) Goodbye, Mother. I'm really sorry. I'll be back as soon as l can.

(BRENDA goes to the front door and opens it. GWEN, her friend, is standing there.)

BRENDA. (*Startled.*) Oh, my God!

GWEN. Hello, Brenda. Remember ME?

BRENDA. Oh, God …

(BLACKOUT.

LIGHTS up on taxi. NICK is driving and SUSAN is now sitting beside him in the front. THEY are sharing coffee from Nick's thermos. THEY're both leaning forward trying to see the road.)

NICK. Jesus H. Christ! Now this is what I call precipitation! I haven't seen anything like this since monsoon season in Thailand in '73. The lightning. The thunder. The wind. And here we are in the home stretch, at the end of the line. Ah, there's nothing like staring down death in the eleventh hour, is there? And there's *nothing* like a blinding rain storm to make you feel alive. Goddamn! I love it! Tearing down the highway. Wipers working overtime. Hydroplaning into oblivion.

SUSAN. (*Joining in.*) Brake lights flashing in the haze up ahead—

NICK —too late to stop.

SUSAN. The sound of brakes squealing.

NICK. A patch of grease in the center lane.

SUSAN. Skidding and fish-tailing—

NICK. —towards a stalled tanker trailer in the middle of the road.

SUSAN. A sickening crash.

NICK. Metal twisting. Glass shattering. Fuel spilling like from an open wound.

SUSAN. A spark. A whoosh.

NICK. Flames lick the sky. Black smoke curls heavenward.

SUSAN. Then, peace. Quiet. And the rain washing it all away … (*SHE stares ahead intently.*)

NICK. (*HE glances at Susan.*) It's up to you. Want to pull over? (*HE gets no response.*) This blinding rain and all—no shame in admitting cowardice. (*HE gets no response.*) You're sure now? (*No response.*) You're sure?

SUSAN. We're almost there.

(*LIGHTS fade to BLACK. In the DARKNESS we hear:*)

NICK. Are you sure you don't want to wait it out? You're sure?

(*LIGHTS up on the living room as before. GWEN is standing in the open door. SHE is wearing a white nurse's pantsuit and a motorcycle jacket. SHE is soaking wet.*)

GWEN Remember me?

BRENDA. Gwen!

GWEN Long time, no see …

BRENDA. You were supposed to wait in the car.

GWEN. The Toyota leaks. I was getting dripped on.

MARGE. Brenda, what's going on, dear?

BRENDA. (*To Gwen.*) I told you I'd just be a minute.

GWEN. I was getting *dripped* on. And that was hardly a minute.

BRENDA. Well, come on. We're leaving.

MARGE. Brenda?

GWEN. (*Entering into the room.*) Without introductions? Is this your family? (*To everyone.*) Hi. Sorry to barge in like this, everyone. I'm Gwen. I'm Brenda's roommate. (*Beat.*) Hi.

BRENDA. Everybody, this is Gwen. We work at the clinic together. She's a nurse, too.

GWEN. Hi, everybody.

BRENDA. I'm giving her a ride to work.

GWEN. Isn't that sweet of her? I can't ride my motorcycle in weather like this.

MARGE. (*To Carol.*) Did she say motorcycle?

GWEN. Brenda has told me so much about you all. And now to finally get to meet you. To actually *meet* you. Face to face. (*Beat, to Brenda.*) Face to face.

BRENDA. Introductions. Yes, of course. (*Quickly.*) Gwen, this is my youngest sister, Anne. And this is my oldest sister, Carol. And that's little Babby our neighbor from next door. And over there is my mother, Mrs. Milhalovic. Everybody, this is Gwen. Say hi, everybody.

EVERYBODY. Hi.

BRENDA. (*Pushing GWEN towards the door.*) Okay? Well, we'd be better dash. We wouldn't want you to be late.

GWEN. (*Pulling away and moving to Marge.*) Mrs. Milhalovic, it's such a pleasure to meet you. I'm sorry to barge in like this. I was supposed to stay in the car. In the rain. In the gloom …

BRENDA. Well, if you would've been patient just one more second.

GWEN. Well, I was getting dripped on.

BRENDA. I was almost out the door.

GWEN. I was getting *dripped* on.

BRENDA. Why don't we talk about this later?

GWEN. Later?

BRENDA. *Much later.*

GWEN. Remember what your therapist said? You're supposed to deal with things as they happen.

BRENDA. Gwen!

MARGE. Therapist?

GWEN. And she was making real progress, too.

MARGE. (*To Brenda.*) You're seeing a therapist, dear?

BRENDA. Just three times a week for the last year, that's all.

GWEN. Actually, it was my idea.

MARGE. Really?

BABBY. Isn't therapy for crazy people?

BRENDA. I really wish you'd stayed in the car, Gwen.

GWEN. I was getting tired of waiting. A person can only wait so long. After that, it begins to breed resentment. (*To Marge.*) Don't you agree, Mrs. Milhalovic?

MARGE. (*Takes a step back.*) Oh heavens, you shouldn't have had to do that. Brenda, where are your manners? Really, I must say ... I don't know what Brenda was thinking of. You shouldn't have had to wait out in the car, (*Trying to recall Gwen's name.*) uh ... uh—

GWEN. —Gwen.

MARGE. Gwen, yes. Gwen! Forgive me, Gwen. It's so hard to keep everyone straight these days. You know how it is.

GWEN. I certainly do.

MARGE. I mean, straight in the sense of confused. What with all these people, I mean. I mean, me. I'm confused. Not you. You're fine, I'm sure. I'm just so sorry you can't stay.

GWEN. Yes, I'd love to meet Susan. Brenda's told me so much about her, too. Something of a mystery, I hear. She hasn't arrived yet?

MARGE. No, not yet. Yes, it's too awfully, horribly, bad you can't stay. Really. Well, we shouldn't keep you. It was terribly nice meeting you, (*Trying to recall Gwen's name.*) uh—

GWEN/BRENDA. —Gwen.

MARGE. Gwen! Yes!

GWEN. (*To Brenda.*) Are we really in a rush?

BRENDA. Yes. Yes, we are.

GWEN. Well, this has been just wonderful. Maybe we can do it again sometime ... weather permitting. Tell Susan hi. I'll meet her another time, I'm sure. And again, I'm so sorry to barge in like this.

MARGE. No problem at all. Goodbye.

BRENDA. Let's go, Gwen!

(Suddenly there is the wail of the tornado SIREN.)

BABBY. The tornado siren. That's the tornado siren!

MARGE. Oh, Shoot!

ANNE. The tornado siren!

BABBY. Oh, my God!

BRENDA. We're supposed to go to the basement.

CAROL. The basement?

MARGE. Yes, we'll have to.

BABBY. Oh, God!

CAROL. Perfect.

GWEN. Should I wait in the car, Brenda?

BRENDA. Don't push it, Gwen.

MARGE. Everyone to the basement.

CAROL. Perfect.

ANNE. I'd better call Tom.

MARGE. No you will not! Everybody let's go. Brenda, you first. Show your friend where to go. Babby, Anne, go on. Carol!

CAROL. It's probably a false alarm.

(The LIGHTS flicker, dim and then go out. The stage is in HALF LIGHT.)

BABBY. Oh, my God! I can't see!

MARGE. Get moving, everyone. I'll get the flashlight and candles and be down in a minute.

CAROL. This could be dangerous, Mom. Let Brenda get that stuff.

BRENDA. Thank you so much.

MARGE. I'll get it. It's my house. I'll get it. Now, go on! Go on!

BABBY. We're all going to die!
CAROL. Oh, for Christ's sake!
BRENDA. Think happy thoughts everybody!

(EVERYONE exits to the basement. MARGE starts for the kitchen.)

MARGE. (*To herself, calming.*) It's a wonderful day. We're all together. It's going to be fine. (*Exits to kitchen.*)

(A moment, then the front door opens and SUSAN, barely discernible, stands in the doorway. There is a flash of LIGHTNING and the sound of THUNDER. MARGE re-enters with the flashlight. SHE sees the figure in the door. SHE stops, startled.)

MARGE. Who's there? Who is it?
SUSAN. Hello, Mother.

BLACKOUT

End of ACT I

ACT II

A moment later. The stage is in SEMI-DARKNESS.

MARGE. (*Pause.*) Susan?
SUSAN. Hi, Mom.
MARGE. (*Long pause.*) Susan?
SUSAN. Yes, Mom, it's me.
MARGE. Susan ...

(SHE takes a step towards Susan. SUSAN takes a step back. MARGE takes a breath. SHE puts her hand on her chest.)

MARGE. Oh, my ... (*SHE sits on the sofa.*)
SUSAN. Mom, are you alright?
MARGE. For a moment I thought it was a ghost, but it's you. Well, don't just stand there, come closer. Come closer so I can see. Closer.

(SUSAN takes a couple of steps in. MARGE shines the flashlight in Susan's face. SUSAN covers hers eyes.)

MARGE. Goodness, look at you. You're really here.
SUSAN. I'm here.
MARGE. Finally, you're here.
SUSAN. Yes, I finally get here and all hell breaks loose, huh?
MARGE. What?

SUSAN. All hell breaks loose ...

MARGE. What do you mean?

SUSAN. The weather. The weather, I mean.

MARGE. Oh, that! I'm not afraid of a little moisture, are you?

SUSAN. I mean, the tornado siren ...

MARGE. This is August, remember? Happens all the time. And anyway, what's a little wind?

(The LIGHTS flicker and come back on.)

MARGE. See? Lights! Nothing to worry about It must be a sign. Everything's going to turn out fine. Just like I've been saying. Now, sit down. Sit down next to me. Shut the door

(SUSAN looks outside.)

MARGE. Shut the door, dear. The rain.

(SUSAN slowly shuts the door.)

MARGE. And why don't you lock it while you're at it? You never know who might be lurking around outside. *(Beat, slowly.)* Lock the door, Susan.

(SUSAN locks the door.)

MARGE. *(Indicating banner.)* So, what do you think? How's the old place look?

SUSAN. *(Still standing. Looking around. Sees banner, fruit boat, etc.)* I hardly expected this ...

MARGE. For you? No trouble at all. Now, you just sit right here. Next to me (*SHE pats the sofa.*)

SUSAN. It was a long drive.

MARGE. Yes, you must be tired. You should sit down. Such a long drive and in this weather, too. (*SHE pats the sofa.*)

SUSAN. (*Still standing.*) Yes.

MARGE. The Farmer's Almanac said bright and sunny for today. Can you believe that? Bright and sunny?

SUSAN. They were wrong.

MARGE. Dead wrong, as usual. I can't imagine why I still read that thing. Not even farmers read that thing anymore. It's no wonder I'm always dressed inappropriately—sweaters when I should be wearing short-sleeves. Wool instead of vinyl. Polyester instead of whatever. (*Pause.*) If you don't sit, I'll have to stand. And I have to tell you, I'm feeling a bit light-headed.

SUSAN. Light-headed?

MARGE. Oh, don't you worry about me, I'm just not used to all this excitement, that's all. We're all thrilled. Everyone's so anxious to see you. Especially, after all this time. All those years.

SUSAN. I was busy …

MARGE. So, would you please sit down? Please?

SUSAN. I need to stretch my legs.

MARGE. If I stand up I'll probably faint in a heap. I know you wouldn't want that, would you? Would you?

SUSAN. No, of course not.

MARGE. Then sit. Next to me—

SUSAN. —Next to you?

MARGE. Right here next to me (*SHE pats the sofa, beat.*) I don't bite anymore, you know.

(SUSAN sits on sofa next to Marge.)

MARGE. *(Pause. Very pleased.)* Oh yes, this is nice. Isn't this nice? Sitting—what a good idea. Let's sit and chat. *(SHE takes Susan's hand.)* Oh, you know what I forgot? In all the excitement? A hug. I forgot your hug. *(SHE hugs Susan long and hard, still hugging.)* Now, it's official. Welcome home. *(Still hugging.)*

SUSAN. *(In the clinch. Pause.)* Mom …

MARGE. *(Still hugging tightly.)* Now, I've got you.

SUSAN. Mom …

MARGE. Oh, I've got you now.

SUSAN. Mom, don't …

(MARGE swings Susan around and cradles her on her lap like a baby.)

MARGE. And I won't let go. *(Cradling her.)* I won't ever let go. Ever, ever, ever.

SUSAN. Mom, stop it. Please. Don't do this.

MARGE. *(Rocking her and holding her tightly.)* Oh, this takes me back.

SUSAN. You're hurting me!

MARGE. I knew everything was going to turn out fine.

SUSAN. I can't breathe!

(MARGE holds tightly. SHE rocks Susan roughly. SUSAN struggles.)

MARGE. Oooooooo, now tell me you love me. Tell me you love me

SUSAN. (*Breaking away.*) Stop it! (*Jumps up.*) You know I hate it when you do that.

MARGE. You always had a problem with affection.

SUSAN. That's not affection. That's not what any normal person would call affection.

MARGE. You never minded wrestling with your father.

SUSAN. Yeah, when I was five years old and *he* always let me win.

MARGE. He cheated.

SUSAN. I think we've better leave Dad out of this, alright? Look, can we have a normal encounter? A conversation? Is that possible? I came a long way to get here.

MARGE. And we're all thrilled about it. I can't help it if I'm a little enthused. (*Pause.*) So, what happened?

SUSAN. What do you mean?

MARGE. "Dire straights …?" If I was your father, I'd say, "How much is this going to cost me this time?" But, I'm more sensitive than that. So, what happened? (*Pause. Slowly, as if to an idiot.*) *To what good fortune do we owe this visit*? Not that it matters. It doesn't. You can tell me anything.

SUSAN. I said, a *conversation*. You're supposed to ease into the interrogation. You're supposed to ask how I am.

MARGE. Oh, I'm sorry. How are you?

SUSAN. I'm fine.

MARGE. You look terribly thin.

SUSAN. I'm fine.

MARGE. And pale. Not that you don't look wonderful. You do. Terribly thin and pale, but wonderful. How was that?

SUSAN. Great. (*Making conversation.*) And how have *you* been?

MARGE. Is there any particular year you're interested in?

SUSAN. Let's say, today. Right now.

MARGE. I'm fine. Can't complain. (*Pause.*) So, what happened?

SUSAN. Mom ...

MARGE. Alrightee. I don't see many of your old friends anymore. Most of them got married. Divorced. A person about needs a score card to keep track anymore ... (*Beat.*) How were the roads?

SUSAN. Some flooding in low-lying areas, but generally pretty good.

MARGE. Long drive, was it?

SUSAN. Very. Luckily, I did get to sleep for part of it, though. Through Pennsylvania.

MARGE. Through Pennsylvania?

SUSAN. In fact, I haven't eaten since Pennsylvania. All of a sudden, I'm starved.

MARGE. You slept *through* Pennsylvania?

SUSAN. You know what I'm craving? Fish sticks.

MARGE. How could you sleep in a moving car through Pennsylvania? I mean, if you were driving?

SUSAN. Fish sticks and ketchup. And French fries.

MARGE. Susan, could you explain this to me, please?

(*There is a KNOCK at the front door.*)

MARGE. Who on earth could that be?

SUSAN. Don't get up.

*(SUSAN goes to the door and opens it. NICK pushes in.
THEY speak confidentially.)*

NICK. Everything alright?

SUSAN. Everything's fine, Nick.

NICK. I was just wondering—

SUSAN. It's fine.

NICK. You've been in here a long time. I wasn't sure
what I was supposed to ... you know ... do.

SUSAN. You were supposed to wait.

MARGE. Susan?

NICK. Yeah well, it's getting pretty nasty out there,
you know?

MARGE. Susan?

NICK. I mean, those sirens and everything ...

SUSAN. Go back to the car, Nick. Just lay on the floor
and lock the doors, if you're nervous.

MARGE. Susan?

NICK. I don't know about this ...

SUSAN. Just do it, please? Please? Please, Nick?

NICK. Okay, it's your nickel.

SUSAN. That's right. Goodbye, Nick. *(SUSAN ushers
him out the door.)*

NICK. You know, since I'm in here and everything,
maybe I should—

(HE whispers to her. SHE leads him in.)

SUSAN. *(Indicating the way.)* It's right through there,
second door on the right.

NICK. (*To Marge.*) I'm sorry to interrupt, ma'am. But, you know how it is ... (*HE shrugs. Sees the banner.*) Oh, isn't that nice? That's really nice. Look at that.

SUSAN. (*Ushering him out of the room.*) Second door on the right. On the right.

NICK. (*In the doorway.*) Again, I'm really sorry. I was supposed to stay in the taxi, but you know how it is. (*HE shrugs, and then to Susan.*) And don't forget now, the meter's still running.

(*HE exits to bathroom. THEY watch him go.*)

SUSAN. There's something about traveling that really gives a person an appetite, isn't there? And there's something about being here, in this house ... I'm craving something deep fried. Because that is what we do around here, isn't it? Eat? Even in the worst of circumstances? Eat? Putter around the kitchen?

MARGE. Susan, who was that person?

SUSAN. Nick.

MARGE. Nick?

SUSAN. Oh, what were those things you used to make?

MARGE. Nick?

SUSAN. You know, with potatoes and lard?

MARGE. Did he say "taxi"?

SUSAN. Tater tots—that's what they were.

MARGE. Taxi?

SUSAN. I WANT SOME TATER TOTS, MOM! I WANT SOME TATER TOTS!

MARGE. Susan, stop it. Stop it right now. I've gone to a lot of trouble to welcome you home. A heck of a lot of trouble. We all have. Anne worked all night on that banner. And Carol helped her straighten it. And Brenda risked her life for some horrible, little green things. And Babby is here. And Brenda's friend what's-her-name is here. And we've all been waiting. We've been waiting all morning for you. All morning plus the ten years that we've been waiting, and it begins to add up. So, I think you owe us something. We're going to have a wonderful party. And you're going to appreciate it. And you're *not* going to act crazy. You're going to act normal.

SUSAN. And what if I can't?

MARGE. And natural. And happy. And relaxed. And nice. And you're going.to smile. And you're going to ask questions. And you're going to seem interested.

SUSAN. But, what if I can't?

MARGE. And we're going to be just the family that we used to be. Before your father died. Before you left like you did. Before everything was blown apart. Before you ruined everything. You're going to make it right again, Susan. You will make it right.

(SUSAN takes a step back. CAROL, ANNE, BRENDA, GWEN and BABBY enter from the basement.)

CAROL. Mom? What's going on? What's happening? (*Sees Susan.*) Susan?

ANNE. It's Susan!

BRENDA. God, Susan!

MARGE. (*Quickly puts on a party hat.*) Surprise! Here's the conquering heroine!

BABBY. Hi, Susan!

GWEN. Hi.

MARGE. Surprise! Surprise!

(SUSAN stands stunned.)

MARGE. Say something, dear. Everybody's waiting.
SUSAN. I'm not ready for this. I'm not …
MARGE. Susan, say something.
SUSAN. I can't. I can't!

(SHE runs out the front door. CAROL and BRENDA go to the door.)

MARGE. *(Calls to Susan.)* Susan! *(To Brenda and Carol.)* Carol, Brenda stay here.
BRENDA. What's going on?
MARGE. Let her go. She's overwhelmed, that's all. Don't worry, she'll be back. She has no place else to go. This time she'll be back. Now everyone, sit! When Susan comes back I want everyone sitting and laughing and listening. We're a family. That's what we do. We love each other. And anyone who has a problem with that can get the hell out right now. I'll throw you out myself. By the seat of your pants, if I have to. Get struck by lightning, for all I care! So, sit down! Right now. Right now. Right … *(SHE slowly sits on the sofa.)* Right … *(SHE takes a breath.)* Right … *(SHE takes a breath.)*
CAROL. Mom?
MARGE. Oh, my … *(Lays her head back on the sofa and closes her eyes.)* You can just get the hell out …
CAROL. Brenda, do something!
ANNE. What's wrong with her?
BRENDA. *(Goes to Marge.)* Gwen, help me.

MARGE. (*Head back, eyes closed.*) Family …
ANNE. Mom? Mom?
MARGE. Goddamn bunch of ingrates …
CAROL. Mom? MOM!

(*NICK enters from the bathroom.*)

NICK. Oh, did I miss the touching reunion?

(*LIGHTS FADE to BLACK.*
Some time later. LIGHTS UP on NICK sitting at the
dining room table singing a country ballad, serenading
the room. ANNE and BABBY also sit at the table.
THEY hang on his every word. SUSAN is still outside.
MARGE is upstairs resting. BRENDA and GWEN are
in the kitchen. CAROL is standing at the foot of the
stairs warily watching Nick. On the table is a coffee pot
and a pitcher of orange juice. ANNE jumps up and takes
a flash picture of Nick. SHE then sits and places the
camera on the table. NICK ends his ballad.)

ANNE. More coffee, Nick?
NICK. You're too kind.
BABBY. More juice?
NICK. Just a swallow more, thanks. I swear, I've died
and gone to heaven and I'm surrounded by angels. So, this
home, huh? It's nice. Very nice. Cosy.
CAROL. How long do you plan on staying?
NICK. As long as it takes, I guess.
CAROL. As long as *what* takes?
NICK. Well, that remains to be seen, doesn't it? Now,
did someone say, "coffee"?

ANNE. Coming right up!

BABBY. Here's your juice, Nick.

NICK. Surrounded by angels …

CAROL. Anne, would you wait by the window and watch for Susan, please?

NICK. I wouldn't worry. She'll be back.

CAROL. Anne? The window?

ANNE. Why?

CAROL. Why? Because I'm waiting over here for Mom. I'm concerned about Mom.

NICK. Now I realize that two years of medical school doesn't qualify me to hang out a shingle, but I know exhaustion when I see it.

CAROL. Oh, you do, do you?

NICK. That's my diagnosis.

CAROL. You wouldn't mind if we got a second opinion, would you?

ANNE. Nick says it's exhaustion.

BABBY. Yeah, Carol.

CAROL. A man of many talents, yet. And here I thought you were just a plain ordinary cab driver.

NICK. Ordinary?

CAROL. Yes, a person who drives people. A chauffeur.

NICK. Best not to jump to conclusions.

CAROL. More like first impressions.

NICK. We do what we have to.

CAROL. What we do is what we are.

NICK. What we are is cumulative.

CAROL. And then we get what we deserve.

NICK. Unless we deserve better. I'm sure you'd agree with that.

BABBY. What are they talking about?

ANNE. Beats me.

CAROL. And a philosopher, too. How unique.

NICK. What do you have a bug up your grass skirt about anyway?

CAROL. Pardon me?

NICK. Acting like an asshole. Treating people like shit.

CAROL. I think you'd better wait outside.

NICK. That's no way to be.

CAROL. I said, outside.

NICK. Excuse me?

ANNE. Not in this weather, Carol.

BABBY. There's still a tornado watch.

NICK. Yeah, I might get blown away.

ANNE. He drove Susan all the way here.

CAROL. That's right. He's a cab driver.

NICK. And the meter's still running, don't forget. Actually, we agreed on a flat fee. But, either way, it does add up.

CAROL. How much does she owe you? I'll write you a check.

NICK. No checks. No credit cards.

ANNE. Carol, don't.

NICK. Cash green.

CAROL. Yes, a cab all the way from New York. Isn't that interesting? Now why on earth would she do that?

(NICK shrugs.)

CAROL. Maybe you'd better tell us what's going on.

NICK. Maybe you better smile and say please.

CAROL. Now look, you wait outside or I swear I'll call somebody.

NICK. Do it.

CAROL. I can have you thrown out of here in two seconds.

NICK. Go ahead.

ANNE. Carol!

CAROL. This is ridiculous. I said, wait outside.

NICK. Make me.

CAROL. What?

NICK. Make me.

CAROL. I can't believe this.

NICK. You look pretty strong. You like to throw your weight around. We could arm wrestle. Or go out to the front yard and mud wrestle. All you have to do is pin me once. All you have to do is … make me.

(NICK stares down Carol. SHE turns away. GWEN and BRENDA enter from the kitchen carrying a large platter of cut-up kiwi. EVERYONE crowds around the platter.)

GWEN. Here we go!

CAROL. Oh, excellent! *More* food …

BRENDA. (*Looking around.*) Susan's not back yet?

CAROL. I think the important thing right now is Mom.

NICK. (*Referring to the platter of kiwi.*) Oh, would you look at that! Now, that's beautiful. What's that in the middle there?

GWEN. It's a radish.

BABBY. All cut up to look like a rose!

BRENDA. Gwen did that.

GWEN. It's for decoration.

NICK. Food art—now there's a real skill.

GWEN. Ever heard of *Le Tete Bleu* in Chicago? My father was the head chef there. He could do amazing things with fruits and vegetables. He would make animals, flowers, faces. When President Reagan ate there once, my father carved his likeness in a musk melon. It was extraordinary.

CAROL. None for me, thanks. I'm not hungry. Susan is MISSING, as usual. My mother is upstairs DYING—

GWEN. She's just tired.

ANNE. See, Carol? Brenda's friend says it's exhaustion, too.

CAROL. Well, what if Brenda's friend is wrong?

BRENDA. Excuse me, but Brenda's friend has a name. It's Gwen. Gwen. Could we all practice and remember that? And she is here with me. Gwen is here with me.

GWEN. Now, *that* is the woman I love.

CAROL. But still, if it *is* exhaustion. Isn't that serious? Don't people get hospitalized for that?

BRENDA. She's resting comfortably, Carol. Just let her be for awhile.

BABBY. Doesn't do any good to worry.

CAROL. Well, that's reassuring coming from a Valium addict.

NICK. No, little Babby's got a point. What you need is your basic, old-fashioned Zen approach—"What is, is." I learned that in the Far East.

CAROL. *The Far East?*

NICK. I met a woman there who took me by the hand and showed me how interesting life can be when you go with the flow—when you wrestle your demons to the ground.

CAROL. *Demons*?

GWEN. Yeah, like when I came here from Chicago? I was so worried that everyone would know I was different. So, I put my leather in the back of the closet, cut my hair in a page boy and bought a Volkswagen.

BRENDA. A Volkswagen?

GWEN. And then finally, I said to myself, "To hell with this. Screw 'em if they can't take reality." You're right—"What is, is." You're damn right.

BRENDA. *I* had a Volkswagen!

GWEN. Now, why doesn't that surprise me?

CAROL. We're missing the point here, people!

BABBY. But everything's so complicated anymore. For example, I was working the express line at the supermarket yesterday? And since it was slow and all, I started reading one of those newspapers—THE INCREDIBLE WORLD ALMANAC? And there was this amazing story, this story about a black man whose skin was turning white who was engaged to this woman who used to be a man. The black man had some pigment disorder or something and the woman had had a sex change. Anyway, it really got me thinking. Nothing is set in stone like it used to be. Everything is gray areas. (*Beginning to get worked up.*) It's no wonder we don't know where to turn. No wonder we lash out in a rage. Because, here we are, hung out to dry, flapping in the wind. Flapping and dripping and damp. I mean, "What is, is"—is fine, if you know what it is exactly. If you know what that is, is. But, nowadays—boy, oh boy, oh boy … (*Takes a Valium.*)

CAROL. (*Beat.*) That's it. I've heard enough. If anybody wants me, *I'll* be outside.

(*CAROL opens the front door. SUSAN is standing in the doorway. SHE enters.*)

SUSAN. Hi, everybody. Miss me?

NICK. Well, if it isn't the guest of honor!

ANNE. Susan! (*Runs and hugs her.*) I knew you'd be back.

SUSAN. Annie!

BRENDA. (*Crosses to Susan and hugs her.*) Well, look at you! Look at you!

SUSAN. Brenda! (*Notices CAROL who has lagged back.*) Hi, Carol.

CAROL. (*Slowly crosses.*) We were worried about you. To run out like that ... to just run away ...

SUSAN. I'm sorry. I needed some air.

BABBY. Well, we've got plenty of that!

SUSAN. Babby?

BABBY. It's me.

SUSAN. Little Babby! How are you?

BABBY. I fell down. And I got married. To Dwight. Remember him? Dwight from up the street?

SUSAN. Dwight ... Torkelson?

(*SUSAN looks at Carol. CAROL looks away.*)

SUSAN. That Dwight?

CAROL. Yes, *that* Dwight.

SUSAN. Sure! How is he?

BABBY. Oh, you know ... (*SHE shrugs.*)

ANNE. Isn't this great? This is so great!

GWEN. (*Getting up.*) I'm Gwen.

BRENDA. Oh Susan, this is my friend, my roommate—

GWEN. —her companion.

BRENDA. Her name is Gwen.

GWEN. Hi.

SUSAN. Hi. (*Looks around.*) Where's Mom?

CAROL. Where do you think?

BRENDA. Worked herself up into a tizzy. Some things never change, do they?

SUSAN. She shouldn't have gone to all this trouble.

NICK. Come on and sit down.

ANNE. Want some coffee?

BABBY. Juice?

GWEN. Kiwi?

SUSAN. So, Mom's alright?

BRENDA. She's upstairs resting.

CAROL. Recovering.

ANNE. The excitement and all.

BRENDA. Don't worry. She'll be fine.

SUSAN. Well! (*SHE sits.*) Here we are! So, how have you all been?

EVERYONE. (*Together.*) Fine.

CAROL. And you?

SUSAN. Oh, fine!

ANNE. I'm pregnant.

SUSAN. Well, congratulations!

ANNE. Number four. I can't wait for you to meet everybody. I mean, you already know Tom, of course.

SUSAN. Tom, yes! How is Tom?

ANNE. Oh … he's fine.

SUSAN. And Brenda you're still a nurse?

BRENDA. I'm working for a clinic now. Women's health services.

GWEN. With me.

BRENDA. With Gwen. We work together.

GWEN. That's where we met.

SUSAN. Really? That's great. And Carol, you're still ... ?

CAROL. Yes, I am. Still.

SUSAN. And you're all here. You're all still here. Still in Ankeny?

ANNE. Yes. Isn't it wonderful?

SUSAN. Yes. And Mom seems ... exactly the same. Hasn't changed a bit.

ANNE. Well, you know Mom. Mom's ... Mom.

(THEY all laugh politely.)

NICK. God, I love small talk!

SUSAN. (*Realizing she's forgotten to introduce Nick.*) Oh, I'm sorry. Everybody, this is Nick.

CAROL. We've met.

NICK. Charming family.

CAROL. Yes, how long are you and Nick staying anyway?

SUSAN. Well, I'm not sure yet. I'm still sorting things out. Looking over my options.

ANNE. Options?

BABBY. Wow.

CAROL. It must be exciting to be so busy. And lucrative, too—what with "options" and all, and taking a taxi all the way here. What is it you do in New York again?

SUSAN. Oh, New York! Oh! So much to do. So many important people doing important things. Always on the run. Never a dull moment.

NICK. You can say that again. I saw a lady jump from the Empire State Building once. Out of the corner of my eye, I saw this bundle fly by in a blur. Landed right on a car. Squashed it flat. You couldn't tell where she ended and it began. Very Zen.

SUSAN. What a fun story, Nick.

NICK. Small talk.

SUSAN. Nick's really a great guy. Really.

CAROL. Is he now?

NICK. You might say I saved her life.

CAROL. Really?

NICK. Aw, t'weren't nothin'.

BABBY. You saved her life? How?

SUSAN. He's speaking metaphorically, aren't you, Nick?

NICK. It was just a little Arab problem.

BRENDA. Arab problem?

SUSAN. It's a long, involved story. Let's not bore them, Nick.

CAROL. *Arab* problem?

NICK. They have this thing about being shot at.

ANNE. Shot at?

NICK. Hot-blooded bunch …

SUSAN. I really don't think they're interested.

BRENDA. Shot at?

CAROL. *Shot* at?

SUSAN. I was aiming at the windows. The bus windows. I told them to sit down. I gave them fair warning.

NICK. Can't imagine why they took it so personally.

SUSAN. Sometimes you have to take control of the situation. We could've suffocated in there.

NICK. You should've seen her hauling down Broadway with that angry crowd in tow. That was some sight! Where'd we toss that gun, anyway?

SUSAN. I really don't remember, Nick.

CAROL. (*Raises her hand.*) Excuse me, gun?

NICK. Jumped in my taxi, put it right to my head and said, "Drive!" (*HE laughs.*) "Drive," she said, like it was a friggin' B-movie. I loved every minute.

SUSAN. He's making it sound a lot more interesting that it actually was. Now, can we talk about something else?

BRENDA. You shot a gun at a bunch of Arab people?

SUSAN. Well, first of all it wasn't my gun. It was my ex-boyfriend's ex-wife's ex-husband's gun. He was an ex-cop. I was going to return it to him. Really. And this occurred in New York, don't forget. New York. And nobody got hurt.

CAROL. And Mom doesn't know?

SUSAN. No, Carol, she doesn't.

ANNE. So, what's going to happen?

BRENDA. Yeah, what's going to happen?

NICK. I'd kind of like to know that myself.

SUSAN. Well, I figured I'd lay low for awhile, and then ... then I'd ... uh ... figure something else out.

CAROL. What ELSE, exactly?

SUSAN. I don't know … exactly. I just need time to figure it out—whatever it is, exactly. Now can we please change the subject? Please?

ANNE. Yes, this is a party, isn't it? Let's put on the hats, why don't we?

BABBY. Oh, boy! A party!

BRENDA. We're going to need some more food. Want to help me, Gwen?

GWEN. Sure.

CAROL. (*Getting everyone's attention.*) Excuse me? EXCUSE ME? So, in other words, we're aiding and abetting and harboring a FUGITIVE? Does that about sum it up?

NICK. The third degree by a rabid CPA.

GWEN. This could get scary.

CAROL. I just want to know what I'm in for. What we're all in for. Legally-speaking.

NICK. Hey! Maybe we could get adjoining cells. Wouldn't that be fun?

SUSAN. Nobody's going to prison, Carol.

CAROL. Oh, no?

ANNE. Prison? I'm pregnant!

BABBY. Dwight was in the drunk tank once. He said it was awful. It was full of drunk people like him. Oh, my God … jail. Barometric pressure—is that a legal defense?

NICK. I bet nobody's ever been in 3x5 bamboo cage in the middle of some jungle hell-hole. Now *that's* awful.

BRENDA. I really think we're over-reacting.

CAROL. For all we know they could've been trailed here. There could be a stake-out going on at this very moment. SWAT teams moving in for the kill. We'll end up on the front page of The Des Moines Register. And to top it off, the icing on the cake—she had the nerve to shoot at an ETHNIC GROUP, which is so politically INCORRECT. Over-reacting? I think not. So, what are we going to do? What? Suggestions? *Options*?

NICK. Well, I'm kind of thinking of California myself.

BABBY. California?

CAROL. There's always the phone, remember. There's always 911.

BRENDA. 911?

BABBY. I think California sounds wonderful.

BRENDA. We can't turn her in, Carol.

(ANNE raises her hand.)

CAROL. (*Calling on her.*) Yes? Anne?

ANNE. I had to get married. I had to. It was supposed to be real hush, hush—only everybody knew about it. That's stupid in this day and age, isn't it?—what with pills and wires and probes and stuff?

CAROL. The topic is "suggestions," Anne, "suggestions."

ANNE. And Brenda has this secret life that we've pretended doesn't exist. Or that she'd get over it. Like a cold or the flu. And Babby's always covered with bruises, that we try not to notice. And Carol, well, there's that little problem with alcohol. Which used to be a bigger problem—when she stopped going to work. Couldn't drag herself out of bed anymore. Until Mom had her hauled off to some clinic. We don't mention that, either.

NICK. Well, my, my …

CAROL. Could we rush headlong to a point, please?

ANNE. We all just kept our dark and sinister secrets to ourselves. So, I think that whatever Susan may have done is her business. Whatever she did is as much a part of who she is as what we've done. What we don't mention. So, what I'm saying ... about Susan ... what I'm saying is— (*Struggling, SHE looks to Nick.*)

NICK. "Misery loves company"?

ANNE. No, not that one, the other one—(*SHE looks to Gwen.*)

GWEN. "Birds of a feather ...?"

ANNE. *That's* what I'm saying. So, I think ... I think we should— (*SHE thinks very, very hard.*)

NICK. Take a vote?

ANNE. *That's* what I'm thinking! A vote! All those who want Susan to stay raise your hands.

(*EVERYONE, but CAROL raises their hands.*)

NICK. Those opposed?

(*EVERYONE looks to Carol. SHE doesn't move.*)

SUSAN. Carol?

CAROL. (*Giving in.*) Oh, what the hell ...

ANNE. Isn't this great? This is so great! So, tell us— (*Sitting SUSAN down in the middle of the sofa.*)

SUSAN. Tell you?

ANNE. We're all dying to know. All that time away ... tell us.

CAROL. You've been an endless source of curiosity for the yokels you left behind.

BRENDA. Start at the beginning.

SUSAN. Well, that's quite a lot …

CAROL. Yes, you all go right ahead. I'll worry about Mom.

ANNE. Maybe just the highlights, then.

BABBY. All the highlights.

GWEN. Everything juicy.

ANNE. Wait! (*Tosses the camera to NICK.*) Nick, would you mind? For the scrapbook?

NICK. My pleasure.

ANNE. (*To Susan.*) Okay, tell us everything.

BRENDA. Everything.

SUSAN. Okay, well— (*SHE thinks.*)

(*THEY move closer.*)

SUSAN. Okay. Uh … well, first I went to St. Louis. (*There is a murmur of interest.*) And then I changed planes for New York. (*More murmurs.*) I did a lot of things to get by. Ten years' worth. It was hard at first. It's always hard to yank up roots. To pack up and go. To create a whole new life. You can do that when you're young and ignorant. When you're young and ignorant the world's a wondrous place. There are so many possibilities. So, you yank up those roots and toss them away like a handful of weeds. Then you blow around for awhile. And time just flies by. And you don't much notice. And you don't much care. And then one morning you wake up in cold sweat, on the hottest day of the year and, well …

NICK. Say cheese, everybody.

EVERYONE. Cheese!

(There is the FLASH of the camera as NICK takes a picture. BLACKOUT. LIGHTS UP on MARGE standing in a pool of LIGHT.)

MARGE. They were tough in those days. They crossed the prairie, don't forget. In covered wagons all the way to get to here. No TVs for them. No VCRs. No fancy electronic distractions. They played cards. They gossiped. They told stories to pass the evening. They had little energy left for anything more. The day began before sun up. You should've seen the breakfasts! Eggs and ham and flapjacks dripping with butter, and bacon and biscuits. We women lived in the kitchen in those times. And nobody was ever late to a meal. And every meal was a brawl. My mother's mother had nine children and they lost all but three to the influenza epidemic that swept through the countryside like a tidal wave. It cut down whole families. The town cemetery had rows and rows of little graves with tiny headstones. Life was abundant and so often short. They don't have epidemics like that anymore. Good, honest epidemics. And there wasn't time to grieve in those days. Everything went on without missing a beat. Drought one season. Flood the next. A savage winter. A late frost. Life hinged on the unknowable. The unpredictable. The only thing you could count on were those around you. Those you could touch and hold and cradle, and when necessary, give a good whack to. Because in those days the family was everything. Something to hold on to. To cling to. To die for. But now ... it's like grabbing smoke ...

(LIGHTS OUT on Marge.

Camera FLASH. LIGHTS UP on the living room, a moment later.)

NICK. That was a nice one. Candid.

SUSAN. I'm sorry, where was I?

NICK. You crossed the prairie in a covered wagon, did you say?

SUSAN. A covered wagon?

NICK. Yes! You braved floods and dust storms and little mealy bugs.

BRENDA. Sunburn.

ANNE. You forded rivers and streams.

BRENDA. You fought indigenous peoples!

BABBY. Arabs!

ANNE. You made—

ANNE/BRENDA. —soap!

GWEN. Soap?

BRENDA. You actually slaughtered a pig and made—

ANNE/BRENDA/BABBY. Soap!

ANNE. And dare we mention the dreaded—influenza epidemic!

BRENDA. Yes! Death meant something in those days.

GWEN. *Soap*?

ANNE. *(To Gwen.)* And everything is nice. It's a nice day. Even Carol's nice.

BRENDA. Even Gwen's nice, once you get to know her.

GWEN. I am?

ANNE. And we're a family. Because that's what we are. A family—

BRENDA. Talking, laughing—

SUSAN/ANNE/BRENDA. Eating.

SUSAN. All that's missing is Dad. Sitting right where you're sitting, Nick, reading the paper. If Dad was here, he'd know what to do.

CAROL. Yeah, the two of you could hop in the car and drive off into the sunset ...

BRENDA. That old Buick!

ANNE. The station wagon!

BRENDA. That wood paneled station wagon!

CAROL. Just the two of you ...

BABBY. (*To Susan.*) I remember you and your dad always going places together. I always thought that was so nice.

SUSAN. Yeah, I'd sit in the car while he sold insurance door to door. For hours I'd wait sometimes. And then other times we'd just drive around and he'd tell the funniest stories!

ANNE. About what?

SUSAN. About lots of things. About ... Mom.

BRENDA. What? What'd he say?

ANNE. Yeah, what?

SUSAN. Do you really want to know?

ANNE. Yes!

SUSAN. Carol?

CAROL. Sure, let's hear it.

SUSAN. He said she talked in her sleep.

ANNE. He said that?

SUSAN. He said her family was quaint—"Hicks from the sticks," he said.

ANNE. "Hick from the sticks"?

BRENDA. I love it!

CAROL. "Hicks from the sticks"? Oh, my God ...

SUSAN. (*Beat.*) He told me she proposed to him.

BRENDA. No!

CAROL. Proposed to him?

ANNE. Mom proposed to *him*?

SUSAN. At a barbecue. She said, "Marry me Bill, or I swear I'll dry up and blow away!"

CAROL. "Dry up and blow away"?

SUSAN. I swear.

CAROL. Dry up and blow away?!

ANNE. Blow away?

BRENDA. At a barbecue?

(THEY laugh. MARGE appears in the doorway.)

NICK. Why don't you join us Mrs. Milhalovic?

(EVERYONE stops laughing.)

MARGE. I wouldn't want to interrupt the festivities.

SUSAN. Mom? Mom, are you alright?

MARGE. Well Susan, you've come back, I see.

NICK. Why don't you sit down, Mrs. Milhalovic?

MARGE. Why thank you, Nick. I just don't want to interrupt all the fun.

ANNE. You're not interrupting anything.

MARGE. Because if there's one thing I hate, it's being a wet blanket.

ANNE. You're not a wet blanket.

MARGE. A party pooper.

ANNE. No, really. You're loads of fun. *(To everybody.)* Isn't she? Isn't she, everybody?

BABBY. Oh yeah, loads and loads.

CAROL. You should be in bed, you know.

MARGE. How could I possibly rest at a time like this? All by myself upstairs? Hearing you all laughing and having a wonderful time down here? Why, I stood at the top of the stairs for the longest time just listening and taking it all in.

CAROL. You did?

BRENDA. I didn't say a word.

ANNE. Me, either.

MARGE. Oh, it took me back! The sound of your voices floating up the stairs. Laughing and whispering. We used to have such wonderful parties, remember? And that comes from my side of the family, because your father's side ... your father's side, well ... They liked to think of themselves as city folks. From *St. Louis,* of all places. Family wasn't important to them. They hardly ever had get-togethers. And when they did, they had picnics. Always picnics. They served fried dough. Lumps of fried dough on sticks. And you've never smelled anything until you've had a whiff of a vat of boiling grease with those lumps of dough bobbing on the top. Pale and big as a man's fist. Bobbing up and down. It made me queasy on more than one occasion, I have to say. They were Baltic or Slavic or something. Or *something.* They themselves didn't have a clue. Can you imagine? Not a clue. Methodists, I believe. We come from good strong Lutheran stock. Nothing fancy. Lutheran Democrats going way back. But, you've heard this a million times, haven't you? Why have an oral tradition when you have TV? Yes, just look at you all. My girls ... huddled together, whispering. Quite a picture, eh, Nick? My right hands ... Carol—the achiever. I could always depend on you to tell me who did what to whom. And Annie, you were always so sweet. Never a lick of trouble. When you were a baby, I could put you down and you'd just sit there for hours until I moved you to the next place. And Brenda, my little helper. If I ever needed anything, I'd only have to look in your direction and off you'd go. Did I mention everybody? Have I forgotten anyone? Oh yes ... Babby. I remember you too, Babby. Always looked like a deer caught in a car's headlights. I figured it was because your father was such a brute. Your mother was a saint to put up with that man. Just like you're a saint to put up with Dwight. And you were always so good to your mother, too, even if you did put her in a home. Oh! But, look at me. Yakking away. It must be these festive vibrations. Gwen, were you nice to your mother?

GWEN. I'm sorry?

MARGE. Your mother? Did you appreciate your mother?

GWEN. Actually, I was raised by my father.

MARGE. Your father? How unnatural!

GWEN. No, it was great.

MARGE. A father could never replace a mother, dear. Never.

BRENDA. Gwen and I stayed with her dad for a weekend. He was wonderful.

MARGE. What about you, Nick? (*MARGE moves to Nick.*) Boys always adore their mothers, don't they? Girls would just as soon knife their mothers in the back the minute puberty strikes.

GWEN. Brenda, could I please wait in the car?

BRENDA. Not on your life.

SUSAN. You forgot to mention me, Mom.

MARGE. I did?

SUSAN. Yes, you did.

MARGE. Oh, how thoughtless of me! Well, let me think back ... Susan ... It was a painful, terrible labor as I recall. It almost killed me. You came out all shrivelled and black and blue. Six weeks premature. But, you were always in hurry, weren't you? Ah yes, Susan—always going off. Going with her father. Going to off to New York. Going off half-cocked. Susan. There? Feel better? And since you *do* want to be part of this family again, on Monday the painters are coming to paint your old room. It's all arranged. A light blue, I think, to match the curtains I picked. Maybe you can get your old job back at the mall. Now, that would be something to celebrate. I feel like dancing, don't you?

SUSAN. This is just a visit, Mom. It's just a quick visit.

MARGE. Really? And here I thought you had no place else to go.

SUSAN. What do you mean?

MARGE. The New York Police were kind enough to call yesterday. It appears they're looking for you. The list of charges is impressive.

SUSAN. You knew this yesterday?

BRENDA. You knew?

ANNE. Mom?

CAROL. You knew and didn't say anything?

MARGE. Because it'll all blow over in time, since no one was hurt, thank God. (*To the room.*) Now, this a party everybody! Let's start having fun! Eat some fruit!

SUSAN. Mom, I said I can't stay. I have to leave.

MARGE. You stop this nonsense right now.

GWEN. Maybe we should *all* wait out in the car ...

SUSAN. I'm sorry.

MARGE. "I have to leave ... " Those were your exact words on the day of your father's funeral. Or maybe you don't remember.

SUSAN. Oh, I remember.

MARGE. Yes, you were wearing a black knit dress. And a black hat with one of those dramatic net veils over your face.

SUSAN. You were wearing a navy, rayon outfit with a pleated skirt. Everyone remarked on how well you were holding up. Just like Jackie Kennedy, they said. It was raining, I remember that.

MARGE. It was bright and sunny.

SUSAN. After the cemetery everyone came back here. So many people, too. Crowding around you. Comforting you. Eating Jello.

MARGE. Spinach dip.

SUSAN. I was on the sofa.

MARGE. You sat in that corner over there on a wooden stool. You just sat there gazing at me.

SUSAN. You kept glancing in my direction.

MARGE. Gazing at me with the strangest look. You told me to come into the kitchen. "I'm not staying, Mom. I have to leave." Your exact words.

SUSAN. And then you said, *you* said, if I go, not to come back.

MARGE. I did not! I did not say that!

ANNE. Is it getting hot in here?

MARGE. I never said that!

ANNE. Could we open a window or something?

MARGE. You had to go away, you said. You *had* to.

SUSAN. I had to.

ANNE. Is anybody else suffocating?

MARGE. He left me, and then you left me. Well, you're not going to do it again. You're not. I won't allow it.

SUSAN. You won't allow it?

MARGE. No.

SUSAN. (*Starting to exit.*) Come on, Nick. Let's go.

MARGE. (*Stopping her.*) It was your father, wasn't it? Your father—telling secrets. Filling your head with foolish ideas about running off to other places. Your father—who couldn't sell insurance to a drowning sailor. I sold my share of the family land to keep us afloat. And I never, ever talked in my sleep. Not one word!

SUSAN. Nick, let's go.

MARGE. I was here for everybody. I kept this family together. So, you're not going anywhere!

SUSAN. (*To the room.*) People! (*Clapping.*) People, if you'll all look this way, you'll see one of the things Susan and her mother are famous for! Well, I'm thirty-one ... thirty-three ... I'm *thirty-five years old* and I don't want to do this anymore. After ten years I thought things would be a little different. (*Starts to go.*) Oh, and just for the record, this party is for me. Me. This is not about *you*. (*To the room.*) I'm sorry, everybody. Come on, Nick.

MARGE. (*Taking a deep breath.*) Oh my, I have to sit. I have to.

(*SUSAN stands at the door. CAROL, ANNE, BRENDA and GWEN go to MARGE and lead her to the sofa.*)

CAROL. Mom, are you alright?

MARGE. Come sit next to me, Susan. (*SHE pats the sofa.*) Let's all forgive and forget.

SUSAN. Nick, are you ready?

MARGE. You don't have anyplace to go, dear. This is your home.

SUSAN. Oh, but I do have another place.

BABBY. California ...

MARGE. And even if I may have said don't come back, I didn't mean it.

SUSAN. No.

MARGE. Susan ...

SUSAN. No!

MARGE. Oh shoot! And I was hoping to avoid this, too ... (*MARGE reaches into her pocket and pulls out a pill bottle.*)

BRENDA. What's this?

SUSAN. What are you doing?

(*BRENDA reads the label, shows it to Gwen.*)

CAROL. What is that?

GWEN. It's heart medication.

ANNE. For what?

BRENDA. For her *heart*, Annie. That's what heart medication is usually for.

ANNE. Her heart?

CAROL. Why didn't you tell us?

MARGE. And be a burden?

SUSAN. Is this true? Really? REALLY?

NICK. (*Indicating pill bottle.*) May I? (*HE takes the bottle and reads the label.*) Yep, heart medication, alright.

ANNE. Oh, God ...

CAROL. Let me see those. (*SHE takes the pill bottle from Nick.*)

ANNE. This is the worst party we've ever had ...

BRENDA. You should've told us.

CAROL. (*Examining the bottle.*) Strange you didn't mention this before ...

MARGE. Would staying here really be so bad?

SUSAN. (*Pause.*) It would kill me.

MARGE. What?

SUSAN. One way or another, it would.

MARGE. Well, it just might kill *me* if you go.

ANNE. I think I'm going to be sick ...

BRENDA. Me, too ...

NICK. May I? (*HE stands.*) I was in a bar fight in Saskatoon once. It was me and this big guy. And I mean, big. Big and dumb, tattoos all up and down his arms. But, I was quick and smart, so I figured it was about even. He'd hit me with something and then I'd hit him with something. Back and forth. On and on. And it was going great! We just kept slugging away. And I was dancing and dodging and swinging and ducking. Didn't even feel a thing, either. And neither did he from the looks of him. And pretty soon I forgot this fight was about something small—he didn't like my boots or my face—something real small like that. We were in the heat of battle. I picked up some heavy thing, don't even remember what it was, and brought it right down on the top of his head. Right square on the top where that soft spot is on babies. Hard as I could. He hit the deck so hard, I knew he wasn't going to get up. He was down for good. And I mean, *good*. I ran out of that bar, jumped in my pick-up and headed south looking over my shoulder the whole way. Been drifting ever since. Anyway, the point being—there's no such thing as a fair fight, not in the heat of the moment anyway. Somebody always has the edge—smarter, faster, stronger, crazier. It's never fair. And somebody always has to lose. Unless, of course ... unless they just walk away. Thank you. (*HE sits.*)

BABBY. What happened to him?

NICK. Beats me.

BABBY. And you got away with it?

NICK. Nobody ever gets away with anything. Not in this life. Not the way I see it. You just try to do things differently the next time and hope that makes up for it. Any more watermelon?

SUSAN. (*To Marge.*) Maybe ... maybe ... I'll write you. And I'll call when I get settled.

MARGE. I'm not loaning you any money.

SUSAN. I don't want your money.

MARGE. Not one penny for this foolishness. And I'm still going to paint your room.

SUSAN. It's not my room anymore.

MARGE. Oh, you'll be back. You'll be back.

NICK. (*Standing.*) Well! This cab's moving out. Better go while there's a break in the clouds. Any takers?

BABBY. Nick, can I go with you? Can I? Please? Please? I have to go. I have to.

NICK. You got any unfinished business you have to take care of?

BABBY. Well ... (*SHE looks nervously towards the front door.*)

CAROL. You might want to see Dwight.

BABBY. Oh yeah, Dwight ...

NICK. Why don't I go with you? Help you pack a few things. I've got lots of trunk space.

BABBY. A lot?

NICK. A whole lot. And I'll take care of Dwight for you.

BABBY. I'd appreciate it.

MARGE. What about your mother?

BABBY. Oh! My mother ... I forgot that too. Marge, would you go see her for me? Talk to her. She won't understand a word you're saying anyway. I hate to ask, but please? Please?

MARGE. Alright, I'll go see her. But, you'll be back Babby. And before too long, I've got a feeling.

NICK. Let's go, then! I've got a lock to pick! Susan, are you coming? (*Offers his hand.*)

SUSAN. (*SHE takes his hand.*) I'll be along in a minute.

NICK. (*To everyone.*) Well, It's been a pleasure, everyone! Yep, a whole novel in just one afternoon. (*HE winks at Carol.*) Maybe, I'll come back sometime, too. Cross your fingers.

BABBY. I'm going to California!

(*BABBY and NICK exit.*)

MARGE. Brenda, you'd better say your goodbyes, too. Your friend's going to be real late for work.

BRENDA. We can't just leave you after all this.

MARGE. You go on now. I'm fine.

BRENDA. (*To Susan.*) Do you have to go? Can't you stay for awhile?

SUSAN. It's now or never, I'm afraid. (*SHE hugs Brenda and Anne, then turns to Gwen.*) Good luck, Gwen. I have a feeling you're really terrific.

GWEN. I am.

BRENDA. She is. Now, you take care of yourself, okay? And don't be surprised if we come visit sometime. Come on, Gwen.

GWEN. Well, goodbye, everybody! Bye, Mrs. Milhalovic. Let's do this again real soon!

MARGE. Yes dear, we'll see ...

BRENDA. (*Pulling GWEN out the door.*) Mom, I'll come by after work and see how you're doing.

(*THEY exit.*)

MARGE. Anne, you'd better get back and see to the kids.

ANNE. I can stay if you want.

MARGE. That's alright.

ANNE. (*To Susan.*) Tom's so inept.

MARGE. Yes, he is.

ANNE. But, I can stay if you need me.

MARGE. I said, I'm fine.

ANNE. I don't mind. Really!

MARGE. Go, Anne. Go! Now!

ANNE. (*Getting teary.*) I love you Susan. (*SHE crosses to the door and opens it.*)

SUSAN. I love you, too.

ANNE. (*In the doorway, really beginning to cry.*) Isn't this neat?!

(*MARGE gets up and crosses to the door.*)

ANNE. Neat and horrible at the same time. I don't know whether to laugh or eat. And someday you'll have to meet Petey and Jane and little—

(MARGE closes the door in Anne's face.)

MARGE. *(Calling to Anne behind the closed door.)* Goodbye, dear! Go home! *(Crossing to sit on sofa.)* Everybody's got one foot out the door most of the time, but the minute you *want* them to leave ... Finally, some peace and quiet. *(Looks to Carol.)* Why don't you say goodbye, Carol. Your sister's leaving, after all.

CAROL. *(Crossing to Susan.)* So, California, huh?

SUSAN. You're welcome to come along.

CAROL. Just pack up and go? Just like that?

SUSAN. Yeah, just like that.

CAROL. Well, I'm kind of settled here now. I've got so much stuff, and there's my career and all ...

SUSAN. Oh, sure ... I understand.

CAROL. You never did tell us what you did in New York.

SUSAN. I was a tour guide.

CAROL. A what?

SUSAN. A tour guide.

CAROL. A tour guide?

SUSAN. Yes.

CAROL. Like, for tours?

SUSAN. Around Manhattan. Bus tours.

CAROL. Oh.

SUSAN. I was very good.

CAROL. Uh huh.

SUSAN. I did it for seven years.

CAROL. On a bus?

SUSAN. Yes.

CAROL. On a *bus*?

SUSAN. Yes.

CAROL. My God ... seven years on a bus? I would've shot the shit out of it long before this.

SUSAN. Thanks, Carol. I know you mean that.

CAROL. Oh, just one last thing— (*Indicating Nick. Whispering.*) Don't fall in love with that guy or anything. Whatever you do. Don't. And don't screw up anymore, okay?

MARGE. Language, Carol ...

SUSAN. You'll take care of Mom?

CAROL. I always have. Well ...

(*CAROL offers her hand. THEY shake. SUSAN hugs her.*)

CAROL. I'm going to get something to eat before I go home. I'll be in the kitchen. (*As SHE crosses.*) Oh! (*SHE hands the pill bottle to Susan.*) These look just like the pills Dad used to take. Exactly like them. Isn't that interesting? Don't talk about me when I'm out of the room, please. (*SHE exits to kitchen.*)

SUSAN. (*Indicating the bottle.*) These were Dad's? These aren't yours?

(*MARGE shrugs.*)

SUSAN. You still amaze me, even after all these years ... (*Sitting on the sofa next to Marge.*) Do you know when I walked through that door this morning I was almost knocked over? Even in the dark the house seemed the same. It smelled the same. And your voice sounded exactly the way I remembered. I felt like I did in high school, after a date, when I'd come home after midnight. Sneaking in. Knowing which floor boards creaked. Knowing you'd be up and waiting. Around the corner or in the kitchen. You always could hear everything. And when I went away, I thought finally, I could do whatever I wanted without looking over my shoulder, or hearing your voice in my head. And it worked for awhile. For awhile, I was overwhelmed. I was distracted. I was far away. As far as I could get. And then slowly things changed. It was like I was swept up in a current, flowing somewhere. Pulled along until I couldn't stay afloat anymore. Until I was drowning. And there was nothing to hold onto. I put the gun to Nick's head that day and said, "Home." He thought I said, "Drive." I said, "Home." And then coming back I started remembering all those stories you'd tell. And when we crossed the state line, I saw the rolling hills, and the cornfields, and the silos, and smelled those horrible pig farms, and was astounded by how green the land was. So amazingly green. So amazingly beautiful. They were tough in those days. They crossed the prairie in covered wagons all the way to get to here. I had to come back. I had to come back so I could leave. Am I making any sense?

MARGE. Nothing makes any sense anymore …

SUSAN. I think I love you, Mom.

MARGE. (*Beat.*) I think I love you too, dear. I think.

SUSAN. Goodbye, Mom. (*SHE starts to go.*)

MARGE. We're not just a pit stop, dear, we're your family.

SUSAN. Take care of yourself. Please?

(SUSAN goes to the door. SHE stops with her back to Marge. Beat. SUSAN exits. MARGE sits very still. SHE looks around the quiet room. SHE seems to listen a moment.)

MARGE. *(Calling to Carol in the kitchen.)* CAROL, SHUT THE REFRIGERATOR DOOR, DEAR! YOU'RE LETTING ALL THE COLD OUT!

(A moment. LIGHTS FADE to BLACK.
A moment, then LIGHTS UP on the taxi. NICK is driving, SUSAN is sitting on the passenger side by the window, and BABBY is sitting between them still wearing her party hat. On her lap is a large radio which SHE holds close. It plays the country tune. THEY happily sing as LIGHTS FADE to BLACK.)

END OF PLAY

COSTUME LIST

Susan   Milhalovic
Navy straight skirt
White blouse with name tag
Long polka dot scarf tied in a bow at the neck
White sheer stockings
Navy pumps
Navy handbag
Nick
Jeans
T-shirt
Bandana (optional)
White socks sneakers
Marge   Milhalovic
Act I
White A-line polyester skirt
Green cotton short sleeve shirt
Flesh-colored stockings
White flats
Flowered ruffled apron
Faux pearl necklace
Act II
Long pink terry cloth bathrobe
Pink slippers
Carol   Milhalovic
Brown slacks with brown belt
Tan blouse
Brown wedge sandals
Ann Cooper
Pastel flowered cotton maternity dress
Pregnancy pillow (eight months)

White canvas slip on shoes
Anklets
Babby Torkelson
White peg leg pants
Sleeveless shirt knotted at the waist
Well-worn leather sandals
Large bracelet
Brenda Milhalovic
Pink and white checked long cotton dress
Beige sandals
Rain poncho
Straw handbag
Gwen Monroe
White nurse short sleeve pantsuit
White nurse shoes
White knee highs
Black leather motorcycle jacket

PROPERTY LIST

TOUR BUS
Gun in handbag for Susan
TAXI CAB
Gun for Nick
Thermos of coffee
LIVING ROOM in IOWA
Food—see below
Bowls for food and candy (Approx. 6)
Melon-baller
Sharp knife
Glasses (offstage in kitchen area)
8 party hats

Pitcher for orange juice
Coffee pot
Coffee cup
Newspaper (The Des Moines Register)
Platter for watermelon
Fruit bowl with kiwi (offstage in kitchen)
Glass of water for Bromo (in upstairs area)
Grocery bag
Towel
Flashlight
Tub of Cool Whip
Spoon
2 pill bottles (one each for Babby and Marge)
Dish rag
Camera with flash
Large portable radio (boom box)

FURNITURE

LIVING ROOM
Small kitchen table
4 chairs
Radio
End tables with lamps on either side of sofa
Coffee table
Small arm chair

FOOD NOTES

Cheese Doodles, Fritos, Potato chips, M&Ms, Watermelon (If out of season a different variety of large melon could be used.), Kiwi—sliced and arranged, Radish—decorative, cut up to look like a rose